For your reading pleasure

CYCLING'S
STRANGEST
TALES

D0240976

For your reading pleasure

CYCLING'S
STRANGEST
TALES

EXTRAORDINARY
BUT TRUE STORIES

IAIN SPRAGG

PORTICO

First published in the United Kingdom in 2014 by
Portico
10 Southcombe Street
London W14 0RA

An imprint of Pavilion Books Group Ltd

Copyright © Portico, 2014
Cover image © Science Museum / Science & Society Picture Library

All rights reserved. No part of this publication may be reproduced, stored
in a retrieval system, or transmitted in any form or by any means electronic,
mechanical, photocopying, recording or otherwise, without the prior written
permission of the copyright owner.

ISBN 9781909396494

A CIP catalogue record for this book is available from the British Library.

20 19 18 17 16 15 14
10 9 8 7 6 5 4 3 2 1

Reproduction by Rival Colour Ltd, UK
Printed and bound by 1010 Printing International Ltd, China

This book can be ordered direct from the publisher at www.anovabooks.com,
or try your local bookshop.

CONTENTS

Introduction   9

The False Pretenders, 1478   12
Fame but no Fortune for the Baron, 1818   14
The Dangers of Pedal Power, 1839   16
How to Avoid a Watery Fall at the Waterfall, 1869   18
Channelling the Power, 1883   20
The Amazing Travels of Thomas, 1884   22
Cycling's Debt to Starley, 1885   25
The Tyre Wars, 1887   28
The Wright Stuff, 1892   30
Answering the Call of Nature, 1893   32
All That Glitters is not Gold, 1896   34
The Last Madison Square Marathon, 1898   36
No Pain no Gain, 1904   38
The Tour's Early Troubles, 1904   40
The Tour's Mystery Man, 1909   42
Christophe Battles The Elements, 1910   44
Duboc's Water Bottle Woe, 1911   46
The Pelissier Protest, 1924   48
Victor Denied Victory, 1929   50
The Big Binda Bribe, 1930   52
Olympic Skullduggery, 1936   54
War on Wheels, 1937   56
A Year in the Saddle, 1939   58
The Bravery of Bartali, 1943   61
Toeing the Line, 1947   63
Chicago Defies Convention, 1948   65
At One with Nature, 1954   67
Not a Pretty Picture, 1956   68
Unbeatable Beryl, 1959   70

Au Revoir, Monsieur le President, 1960   72
Cycling on the Curriculum, 1961   74
The Idiocy of Inertia, 1965   76
The White Bike Man, 1965   78
Out of this World, 1973   80
BMX Gets a 'Bum' Deal, 1974   81
Luck of the Irish Runs Out, 1975   83
The Breakaway that Backfired, 1978   85
Hoy's Debt to Hollywood, 1982   87
Morgan's Beastly Leap, 1982   89
Into the Valley of Death, 1983   91
The Global Dash, 1984   93
'Look, No Hands!' 1985   95
Onward Christian Soloist, 1988   97
'St Michael' to the Rescue, 1990   99
Stairway to Heaven, 1993   101
Women, Wheels & Politics, 1996   102
Two Wheels Versus Four Legs, 1997   104
An Unlikely Medical Hero, 2000   106
Sir Bradley's Vegetarian Porkies, 2001   108
Manser's African Odyssey, 2003   110
The Numbers Game, 2004   112
Muddying the Waters, 2005   113
The Fold-away Phenomenon, 2006   115
Who Let the Dogs Out? 2007   117
The Love that Dare not Speak its Name, 2007   119
You've Been Framed, 2007   121
Plumbing New Depths, 2008   123
The Madness of Sir Dave, 2008   125
Ain't no Sunshine Any More, 2008   127
Going for Gold, 2008   129
Copenhagen's Congested Claim to Fame, 2008   131
Rising to the Occasion, 2008   133
The Summit of Cycling, 2009   134
Bobbies on Bikes, 2009   136
It'll All Come Out in the Wash, 2009   138
Batteries Not Included, 2010   140

Brought Down to Earth, 2011   142
The Height of Ingenuity, 2012   143
The Big Chill, 2012   145
Play Your Card Right, 2012   147
Just Married! 2012   149
Jamie's Road To Nowhere, 2012   151
Carry On, Doctor, 2012   153
Froome's African Adventure, 2013   155
The Sky's The Limit, 2013   157
The Need For Speed, 2013   159
Shanghai High Rise, 2013   161
The Bicycle Bandits, 2013   163
It's not Always Good to Talk, 2013   165
Canadian Cardboard Caper, 2013   167

Bibliography   170

INTRODUCTION

'As a kid I had a dream,' John Lennon once said. 'I wanted to own my own bicycle. When I got the bike I must have been the happiest boy in Liverpool, maybe the world. I lived for that bike. Most kids left their bike in the backyard at night. Not me. I insisted on taking mine indoors and the first night I even kept it in my bed.'

The late, great Beatle was, of course, just one of a global army of cyclophiles. With an estimated billion or so bikes in the world today, cycling has never had it so good in terms of bums on seats and tyres on tarmac and whether it is a lazy, recreational pedal or lung-busting cyclo-cross action, from the thrills of BMX to the drama of the Tour de France, cycling is both one of the world's most popular pastimes and fastest-growing sports.

Cycling's Strangest Tales charts the weird and wonderful evolution of the bicycle, the eccentric and controversial characters who have helped pioneer and popularise cycling and the oddest examples of two-wheeled mayhem on the planet.

It was back in the early 19th century that the German inventor Baron Karl von Drais first unveiled his 'laufmaschine' ('running machine'), the widely acknowledged template for the modern bicycle, unwittingly sparking a global phenomenon which shows absolutely no sign of abating.

Drais' wooden-framed contraption with two in-line wheels had no pedals and failed to make its designer his fortune – but his invention certainly made an enduring impression on an unsuspecting world in ways he probably could never have envisaged in his wildest dreams.

The pages that follow will explore the full gamut of surreal cycling stories and prove there really are absolutely no limits to what people will attempt given access to a saddle or two, handlebars and two good wheels.

Many of our strange tales focus on the world of endurance riding and extreme cycling; ever since Thomas Stevens first successfully pedalled his way around the globe in the late 19th century, cyclists have been going faster, further and higher. Italy's Vittorio Innocente even managed to pedal away at a depth of 65m (213ft) underwater, while honourable mention must also go to astronaut Alan Bean, the first man to hop into the saddle in space.

The bizarre tale of the Polish cyclist who spends his spare time pedalling up the world's tallest skyscrapers has to be read to be believed, while the story of a two-wheeled assault on the South Pole is a timely reminder that the human spirit of adventure is very much in rude health.

Professional cycling may be more glamorous (and profitable) than its amateur cousin but that doesn't make it a less rich source of unexpected anecdotes. From the moment money was at stake, racers have gone to increasingly nefarious lengths to ensure they were the first over the finishing line.

The Tour de France, for example, has seen riders amputating their own toes, the poisoning of rivals, surreptitious train rides and rioting on the streets in its long and sometimes chequered history. Other professional events have stood unwitting witness to shameful acts of bribery and corruption, an unexplained consignment of Viagra and an inner tube brimming over with urine.

You will also have to read on to discover when Chris Froome's career was almost cut short by an angry hippopotamus, how Sir Bradley Wiggins' carnivorous tendencies nearly ruined his cycling dreams and why Sir Chris Hoy really owes it all to Steven Spielberg.

The bicycles themselves, however, remain the real stars of the show and *Cycling's Strangest Tales* is replete with stories of the most unusual models and modifications on Drais' original, ground-breaking vision. Whether it is the American bike bristling with 13 shotguns welded to the frame, the cycle that can actually soar into the sky or the two-wheeler designed by Damien Hirst that sold for an eye-watering £325,000, we've got them covered.

It is also true to say that cycling has always attracted more than its fair share of eccentrics. Those who compete in the annual World Mountain Bike Bog Snorkelling Championship in Wales are certainly not what you'd call conventional cyclists, while the suited and booted competitors at the Brompton World Championships every year are verging on the bonkers. Why anyone would devote themselves to the 'art' of pedalling backwards while playing the violin will forever remain a mystery, and the Scottish gentleman inadvertently caught in an overly amorous embrace with his bike in 2007 was, we can surely all agree, simply deranged.

Bicycles of course are designed to get their riders from A to B without the inconvenience of walking but they have frequently been pressed into alternative service and at various times our two-wheeled friends have played their part in invading China and doing the laundry, jumping over elephants and catching criminals. You can even make ice cream on a bike.

Cycling's Strangest Tales follows the colourful 200-year history of the bicycle and its legion of devotees with a mixture of reverence and amusement, proving that the writer H. G. Wells definitely had a point when he observed, 'Every time I see an adult on a bicycle, I no longer despair for the future of the human race.'

THE FALSE
PRETENDERS
1478

To tell the story of the evolution of cycling, we must, of course, begin with the beautiful bikes themselves. Without them, this would be a disappointingly brief book and millions, perhaps billions of people would have to find alternative forms of both transport and recreation.

There is, though, an initial problem in the recounting of the bicycle's fascinating history. We must first debunk the spurious but frequently repeated paternal claims of two inventions which have for too long tried to ride the bike bandwagon.

The first false claimant as the original bike focuses on a sketch allegedly penned by the one and only Leonardo da Vinci. It appears in his celebrated collected work *The Codex Atlanticus*, a huge compendium of his writing and drawings dating from 1478 to 1519, and to be fair, it definitely looks like a bike. Two wheels, pedals, a seat, the full monty.

The sketch was discovered in the 1970s when the *Codex* was being restored by Italian monks and what with Leonardo being widely regarded as a bit of a genius, everyone assumed it was safe to add 'inventor of the bicycle' to his already impressive CV.

But then the doubts surfaced and by the 1990s most historians and experts accepted the suspiciously prophetic diagram was not exactly kosher.

'News of a bicycle-like sketch said to have been discovered during the ten-year restoring period of Leonardo da Vinci's *Codex Atlanticus* popped up in 1974, when literary historian Augusto Marinoni gave a lecture in Vinci, Leonardo's birthplace,' explained Prof. Dr. Hans-Erhard Lessing at the eighth International Conference on Cycling History. 'From the chronology of disclosures and evidence, it is now becoming clear that we are dealing with a recent forgery.'

We don't know who 'added' the sketch of the bike but it was not da Vinci. Unfortunately the *Codex* is now encased in plastic to preserve it for posterity and the results of a carbon-dating test on the paper have never been made public.

The conspiracy theorists have had a field day and the finger of blame has variously been jabbed at a pupil of Leonardo, a monk with a wry sense of humour who undertook the restoration work and even Marinoni himself. The more prosaic truth is we may never know.

The second imposter is a contraption dubbed the 'célérifère', allegedly invented by a chap called Comte Mede de Sivrac and apparently unveiled to an eager French public in 1790. A wooden framed design boasting two wheels, a rudimentary seat but lacking handlebars to steer, it's a plausible if erroneous claimant but it was not until the 1970s that the célérifère was exposed as a false prophet.

The research revealed that de Sivrac was no more than an invention by French journalist Louis Baudry de Saunier in the late 19th century and the mythical célérifère no more than a patriotic hoax, an attempt to give a Frenchman the credit for giving the world the bicycle. Perhaps de Saunier can take comfort from the fact that even today there are plenty of Internet sites that continue to be taken in by his hoax.

FAME BUT NO FORTUNE
FOR THE BARON
1818

Now that we have exposed the twin charlatans that are da Vinci's drawing and the célérifère, the burning question remains who the hell did invent the beloved bicycle? Who first came up with the beguilingly simple idea of mounting a couple of wheels on a frame and making a mockery of walking from A to B?

The truth is there was no single 'Eureka moment'. It's a story of evolution not revolution, of refinement and development rather than a fully-formed birth but most historians agree that the first authentic, totally legit forerunner of the modern bike was the '*laufmaschine*', a machine invented by the ill-fated German, Baron Karl von Drais.

Also known as the 'velocipede', the wooden machine featured two wheels in tandem, a seat for the rider and a steering column. Pedals were yet to make an appearance in our story of the bicycle and riders propelled themselves forward by pushing off from the ground with their legs.

After taking his invention for a couple of test rides, von Drais exhibited it to the public in Paris in 1818 and everyone was frightfully impressed. He was the toast of the French capital and as the popularity of the velocipede steadily grew, he began to dream of the riches his ingenuity would bring.

He had, of course, overlooked one small thing. There were no patent laws to speak of in either France or his native Germany back then and once he had publicly shown his hand, there was precious little he could do to prevent anyone copying and modifying his original design. They say imitation is the sincerest form of flattery but that's cobblers when you're trying to earn a living.

The latter years of von Drais' life were as turbulent as they were tragic. A political murder and his father's position as a leading provincial judge forced him to go into self-imposed exile in Brazil in 1822 and his fortunes did not improve significantly on his return to Germany five years later.

He headed to his hometown of Karlsruhe in the Baden region but it was an area in the grip of simmering revolt and rebellion and in 1849 fighting broke out between Republican rebels and the controlling Imperial forces of Prussia. Poor old von Drais publicly sided with the Republicans and when Prussia eventually emerged victorious from the regional squabble, they bankrupted him as punishment.

He died a penniless man just before Christmas in 1851, his *laufmaschine* never earning him either the recognition or the hard cash he deserved. Generations of cyclists however remain indebted to the unlucky German.

THE DANGERS OF PEDAL POWER
1839

The early bikes, inspired by Karl von Drais's design, were all well and good but they lacked a fundamental *je ne sais quoi*. Without pedals, they were akin to a potential masterpiece awaiting the final stroke from the artist's brush and, frankly, riders looked ridiculous pushing themselves along like frantic frogs.

The bike's prayers were finally answered in 1839 by an enterprising Scottish blacksmith by the name of Kirkpatrick MacMillan and once he'd welded on a couple of well-placed pedals, cycling finally had lift off.

The idea for pedals hit MacMillan when he began working as a blacksmith's assistant for the Duke of Buccleuch at Drumlanrig in Dumfriesshire. He noticed the inelegance of the people on their passing velocipedes and soon set his mind to finding a solution to the problem of propulsion and riders' incessant need to put their feet on the ground.

After a couple of dead ends, he had it. 'This first pedal bicycle was propelled by a horizontal reciprocating movement of the rider's feet on the pedals,' reads MacMillan's profile on the BBC website. 'This movement was transmitted to cranks on the rear wheel by connecting rods. The machine was extremely heavy and the physical effort required to ride it must have been considerable. Nevertheless, Macmillan quickly mastered the art of riding it on the rough country roads and was soon accustomed to making the fourteen-mile journey to Dumfries in less than an hour.'

Top work, fella, but even greater challenges lay ahead and in June 1842 MacMillan embarked on a remarkable 70-mile journey from his home to Glasgow to put his new bike through its paces. It got him to the city but the ride climaxed in the worst possible way when he knocked over a young girl in the Gorbals.

A Glasgow newspaper reported the following day how a 'gentleman from Dumfries-shire who bestrode a velocipede of ingenious design' had hit the girl and was fined five shillings. Thankfully she escaped with minor bruises but cycling had just witnessed its first reported crash.

It would be remiss at this point not to concede some historians are sceptical of the whole MacMillan story but the weight of scholarly opinion remains behind our inventive Scottish blacksmith and his penchant for pedals.

For the record, the doubts relate to a chap named James Johnstone, who was MacMillan's nephew. Johnstone was anxious his uncle's achievement had been overlooked and at the 1896 Stanley Show, he exhibited a replica of his bicycle in the hope of securing MacMillan's rightful place in the cycling annals.

The problem was the design he used actually belonged to a cartwright called Thomas McCall, who built two velocipedes of his own, complete with pedals, in 1869 and also manufactured the Stanley Show exhibit on behalf of Johnstone.

It's an interesting theory but does beg the question why McCall would work for a man who was publicly trying to expunge him from the history books.

Like von Drais before him, MacMillan never enjoyed great financial rewards for his innovation but that was because he never filed a single patent application or tried to sell his bike commercially, which is also why the sceptics suspect he may not be our man. They ignore, of course, the possibility that MacMillan simply was not cut out for a 19th equivalent of *Dragon's Den*.

HOW TO AVOID A WATERY
FALL AT THE WATERFALL
1869

The Niagara Falls are like a magnet for madmen, sorry, intrepid daredevils who never seem to tire of devising dangerous and demented ways of crossing the cascade that separates Ontario in Canada and New York in the States.

It all started in the summer of 1859 when Frenchman Charles Blondin decided he was tired of life and determined to tiptoe across the gorge on a tightrope. Remarkably, he didn't die, and ever since then suicidal stuntmen and women have been throwing caution to the wind and traversing the Falls.

It was, of course, merely a matter of time before someone attempted to make the crossing on a bike on a tightrope and the honour was to fall to a fella called Andrew Jenkins. Born in Gloucestershire, Jenkins emigrated to Canada in his childhood, and at the age of 15, his dad took him to see Blondin's spectacular stunt. Jenkins resolved he simply had to conquer Niagara himself. On two wheels.

His big day came in August 1869, and after securing a 10cm (4in) diameter rope across his chosen 320m (1,000ft) span, he readied himself for his leap of faith.

'A new candidate has made his appearance before the public for glory, renown and shekels,' reported *The Buffalo Express* the following day.

> He is called 'Professor Jenkins' or 'the Canadian Blondin' and his forte is riding the bicycle on a rope. Early in the day the crowd around the falls was far from small, and by noon the excursion trains on the Great Western and Lake Huron

Railroads had brought thousands of people, all anxious to see the man ride over the falls on the velocipede.

'At 2.30 o'clock the Professor made his appearance at a small house on the Canada side with the pieces of his machine, and at once proceeded to put them together, a task of no small labour. All being in readiness, the bicycle was fastened by a rope to the bank.

'He wore white tights, black velvet knee breeches, shoulder straps and cross belts of the same material, and on his head was placed a crown-shaped hat and all were profusely bedecked with tinsel and beads. His feet were covered with buff moccasins.

'Three pistol shots were then fired from the Canadian side and it was a 'Go'. The machine moved slowly forward, the rope swaying gently from side to side until he had passed about 50 feet, when another opportunity was given the artist, after which he crawled along at a snail's pace to the middle of the abyss, where he raised and waved his hat and received a faint cheer in response.

'From the center to the American shore it was evidently hard work to propel the bicycle, but at last the edge of the cliff was reached, and then the welcome did ring with the applause of the people. The time occupied in passing over the rope was just 11 minutes.

The 'Canadian Blondin' was pushing it considering his English heritage but he had made it across unscathed and fulfilled his childhood dream. Jenkins traversed the Niagara Falls just that one time but cashed in on his new-found fame for the next 15 years, performing a similar high-wire act across, amongst other places, the Rocky River in Ohio.

Jenkins' challenge may sound surreal but his effort was positively sane compared to the exploits of Maria Spelterini seven years later when the Italian tight roped across the Falls firstly with her feet strapped into fruit boxes and then blindfolded. Miraculously, she made it safely over on both occasions.

CHANNELLING THE POWER
1883

The very essence of cycling is pedal power but if you've ever piloted a pedalo, you'll be aware that you can also make waves on the water. Pedalling can get you from A to B on dry land but with the right rigging and a life jacket, you can also sail the Seven Seas with a spot of good old-fashioned legwork.

This duality was not lost on one William Terry back in 1883 when he made one of the earliest attempts to create a truly amphibious vehicle and cross the English Channel for a spot of Duty Free shopping.

Young William began his journey on a tricycle in London and when he arrived in Dover, he hopped off, mounted the bike on top of a canoe and fixed paddle wheels to the rear axle. It wasn't quite as sophisticated as James Bond's white Lotus Esprit in *The Spy Who Loved Me* but the contraption did work and after 20 gruelling hours of pedalling, Terry eventually made it to France.

Legends has it that he was collared on landing by les gendarmes, who were convinced he was a smuggler, and was only allowed to continue his onward journey to Paris after quite reasonably pointing out he'd have to be unbelievably brazen, not to say bonkers, to commit such a crime on a canoe-mounted tricycle.

Terry did, however, open the floodgates for similar cross Channel tomfoolery and in 1929 Aimee Pfanner made it from Continental Europe to dear old Blighty on what was known as a 'hydro-cycle', a regular bike frame mounted on two long floats and powered by paddle pedals.

It took our plucky French girl around 14 hours to complete her journey, contemporary newspaper reports solemnly telling their readership that 'during the trip she ate food, chiefly fruit.'

One of the fastest pedalled-powered jaunts from England to France came in 1962 when two chaps called Ronald Brooks and James Wood fixed a tandem onto floats. They surged their way across in just eight hours and 55 minutes, proving the old *1984* mantra 'Four legs good, two legs bad'.

THE AMAZING TRAVELS OF THOMAS

1884

The sense of adventure and pioneering spirit has been a hallmark of the British character for centuries and ever since the likes of Sir Walter Raleigh and James Cook set sail in search of mythical lands and profitable new territory, Brits have been travelling the globe frequently armed with little more than a stiff upper lip, immaculately ironed shirts and a haughty disdain for the indigenous population.

In the world of cycling, Blighty has arguably never produced a more marvellous adventurer than Thomas Stevens, the first man to circumnavigate the globe on a bicycle. That's right, right around the whole ruddy world on two wheels.

Stevens' remarkable journey began in the United States in 1884. His original plan was to become the first to pedal across North America and once he had acquired a 127cm (50in) Columbia 'Standard' penny farthing for the challenge, he was good to go and at eight o'clock on 22 April, he set off from San Francisco.

According to the *Adventure Cyclist* magazine, our intrepid cyclist was as tanned as a nut and 'a man of medium height, wearing an oversized blue flannel shirt over blue overalls, which were tucked into a pair of leggings at the knee'. They added, 'A mustache protruded from his face.' He travelled light, packing his handlebar bag with only spare socks and a shirt, a raincoat which doubled as a tent, his bedroll and (just in case) a 38 Smith and Wesson revolver.

Following wagon trails, railways and the public roads, he made superb progress and on 4 August, he triumphantly pedalled into Boston to complete his unprecedented 5,955km (3,700 mile) trek.

'More than one-third of the route followed by Mr. Stevens had to be walked,' reported *Harper's Weekly*. 'Eighty-three and a half days of actual travel and twenty days stoppage for wet weather made one hundred and three and a half days occupied in reaching Boston. He followed the old California trail most of the way across the plains and mountains, astonishing the Indians, and meeting with many strange adventures.'

He was not finished yet. After spending the winter in New York he took a boat to England and prepared to get back in the saddle once again, setting off from Liverpool on 4 May 1885.

'A small sea of hats is enthusiastically waved aloft and a ripple of applause escaped from 500 English throats as I mount my glistening bicycle,' Stevens reminisced in the account of his epic adventure, *Around the World on a Bicycle*. 'With the assistance of a few policemen, 25 Liverpool cyclers who have assembled to accompany me out extricate themselves from the crowd, mount, and fall into line two abreast and merrily we wheel down Edge-lane and out of Liverpool.'

He caught a ferry from Newhaven to Dieppe but Continental Europe posed him few problems and he pushed on to Persia, where he spent the winter in Tehran as the guest of the Shah. His reputation, it seemed, preceded him.

There were, of course, obstacles along the route. There was the near-constant threat of an unwelcome contretemps with bandits, he was refused permission to cycle through Serbia, he was kicked out of Afghanistan by the local authorities after a little misunderstanding and he had to be given refuge from rioters in China when he inadvertently stumbled into a spot of local bother.

He was, however, nothing if not persistent and on 17 December 1886, he reached Yokohama in Japan. His days of pedalling were over, as he dryly noted in his book. 'Distance actually wheeled,' he wrote, 'about 13,500 miles.'

Stevens' adventuring days were not quite over and after an invitation by the *New York World* newspaper in 1888, he set off on an expedition to find the AWOL explorer Stanley in East Africa. He also jaunted off to Russia and sailed the rivers of Europe before returning to Britain, getting married and enjoying the rather more sedate pace of life that came with his job as the manager of the Garrick Theatre in London.

There is yet one more footnote to this amazing story and that's the fate of Thomas' trusty penny farthing. After finishing his marathon in the saddle in Japan, he sailed back to San Francisco in January 1887 and the bike was bought by the famous cycle manufacturer, The Pope Company.

They diligently preserved the record-breaking machine for over 50 years but committed cycling history sacrilege when the Second World War broke out, donating Stevens' indefatigable companion to a scrap-metal drive. Despite its questionable suspension and dubious ride comfort, the old Columbia 'Standard' deserved better.

CYCLING'S DEBT
TO STARLEY
1885

We have just shared the amazing story of Thomas Stevens' jaunt across the globe on his faithful Columbia 'Standard' (see The Amazing Travels of Thomas, page 22) but the truth is the first generation of penny farthings were an absolute bugger to ride.

Perched precariously 1.5m (5ft) in the air, the rider required the balance of a Bolshoi ballerina to avoid toppling over and the leg power of Sir Chris Hoy to get the unwieldy contraption moving and was generally about as safe as Greek Government bonds.

In short, the cycling revolution desperately needed a more manageable machine.

'However enthusiastic one may have been about the ordinary [penny farthing],' wrote the journalist W.F. Grew in 1921, 'there is no denying that it was only possible for comparatively young and athletic men, and if it had remained the only bicycle obtainable, the pastime and the utility of cycling would never have reached its present state of popularity.'

Step forward John Kemp Starley, the man widely credited with providing the much-needed template for the modern bicycle.

Born in London in 1854, Starley moved to Coventry at the age of 18 to work with his inventor uncle. Five years later he met local cycling enthusiast William Sutton and the new chums decided to go into business, forming the somewhat prosaic Starley & Sutton Co.

The dynamic duo initially built tricycles but with the mantra that 'two wheels are better three' ringing in their ears, they turned their attention to how to solve a problem like a penny farthing. They rebranded the company in 1883 as Rover and two years later they were ready to change the history of cycling.

They unveiled their creation in 1885 at the Stanley Cycle Show in London, Britain's main annual bicycle exhibition. They called it the Rover Safety Bicycle and to say it was a hit with the public would be an understatement.

The big deal was, of course, the design. Featuring two nearly equal-sized wheels, there was a hell of lot less chance of falling off. It was a rear wheel drive, a significant departure from the old penny farthings. The front forks directly steered the bike. You didn't need to be an Olympic gymnast to pilot one.

'I felt the time had arrived for solving the problem of the cycle,' Starley explained in a lecture more than a decade after his invention was unveiled. 'I therefore turned my attention solely to the perfection and manufacture of the Rover bicycle.

> 'The main principles which guided me in making this machine were to place the rider at the proper distance from the ground, to place the seat in the right position in relation to the pedals, and to place the handles in such a position in relation to the seat that the rider could exert the greatest force upon the pedals with the least amount of fatigue.
>
> 'My aim was not only to make a safety bicycle, but to produce a machine which should be the true Evolution of the Cycle, and the fact that so little change has been made in the essential positions, which were established by me in 1885, proves that I was not wrong in the cardinal points to be embodied to this end.'

The new Rovers flew off the shelves and it was not long before manufacturers across the world were copying Starley's basic design. The 'modern' bicycle had been well and truly born.

The man himself died in 1901 aged just 46 but his legacy in the world of cycling remains unquestioned.

'His Rover Safety revolutionised not just the bicycle but the world,' said Phillip Darton, the executive director of The Bicycle Association of Great Britain, in a 2012 interview. 'The billions of bicycles made since 1885 can trace their ancestry back to that original ground-breaking machine.'

A fascinating if treacherous footnote to Starley's story is the fact the Rover company began manufacturing motorcycles and cars three years after his premature death, hardly a touching tribute to the man who founded the company and devoted so much of his life to pedal rather than petrol power.

THE TYRE WARS
1887

The human spine is a remarkable bit of biological engineering but as many are painfully aware, it can be utter agony when something goes wrong with all those delicate, temperamental vertebrae. In a recent completely made-up survey on the nation's biggest annoyances, back pain came in ahead of the VAT man, adverts for webuyanycar.com and Spanish air-traffic controllers.

Spare a thought then for the poor folk who were forced into the saddle in the early days of cycling when the luxuriously pneumatic tyre was but a distant dream and shattered spines were all too commonplace.

The forerunner of the inflatable tyre we know and love today was an unforgiving band of iron moulded around a wooden wheel and while this did offer a degree of protection to the fragile inner wheel, no such courtesy was extended to the equally fragile derrière of the rider who greeted the sight of a cobbled street with the same enthusiasm a condemned prisoner welcomes the firing squad.

In 1887, however, cycling learned the name of its saviour. The new messiah was Scotsman's John Boyd Dunlop who, after spending 10 years working as a vet, turned his considerable intellect to the thorny issue of his son's maddeningly uncomfortable tricycle and, hey presto, he invented the inflatable tyre. It probably wasn't quite that straightforward but you get the picture.

Dunlop applied for a patent in 1888 and when Irish cyclist Willie Hume became the first rider to win a few races on a bike with the new-fangled pneumatic tyres at a meeting in Belfast, the world sat up and took notice.

Except Dunlop *didn't* invent the pneumatic tyre. To be fair, he thought he was the first man to champion the comfort of cyclists' backsides but at this stage of the story we must introduce Robert

William Thomson, a fellow Scot who actually beat Dunlop to the punch by some 42 years.

Thomson hit on the idea of an inflated inner tube protected by a durable rubber 'outer' in the 1840s. He was granted a patent in France in 1846 and in the USA in 1847 and later that year he exhibited his 'Aerial Wheels' in action on a horse-drawn carriage in Regents' Park in London. When his new invention failed to make his fortune, Thomson contented himself with working for a sugar-cane company in Java, as well as trying to perfect a self-filling fountain pen, before returning to Scotland and dying in 1873. When the assignees of his patent heard of Dunlop's development they protested to the relevant authorities and the 'second' patent was withdrawn in 1890.

Dunlop sold his now seemingly worthless patent to an English entrepreneur called Harvey du Cros in 1896 for what proved to be a modest £3,000. Du Cros formed the Dunlop Pneumatic Tyre Company and he went on to earn a considerable packet from the Dunlop rubber brand.

Dunlop, meanwhile, died in Dublin in 1921. He was far from a pauper when he passed away but, like Thomson, must have felt a little, ahem, deflated that his idea never made much of an impact on his bank balance.

THE WRIGHT STUFF
1892

The names of Orville and Wilbur Wright are indelibly associated with the invention of the aeroplane and the maiden flight of their famous 'Wright Flyer' back in 1903. It's a cracking claim to fame but it's often scandalously overlooked that the boys cut their mechanical teeth repairing and designing bicycles. In fact, the bicycle also played an important role in the first plane engine.

It was in 1892 that the brothers founded The Wright Cycle Company in Dayton, Ohio. Like any good businessmen, they quickly expanded into renting and selling bikes as well as fixing them and it wasn't long before they began designing them too.

Their 'Van Cleve' and 'St. Claire' models were unveiled in 1896. They were successful enough but it was the priceless experience the Wrights gleaned from the engineering process that was to prove crucial to their later work.

Oh and the money, which they took out of the company and invested in a homemade wind tunnel where they could indulge their growing fascination with air travel. The boys were getting closer to their date with destiny.

There remained, however, one big problem. They had designed and built the Flyer's frame, they were happy enough with the angle of the wings and they'd found a dashing pair of goggles to wear. Their big headache was the engine and, unable to source a suitable car engine for the job, they commissioned Wright Cycle Company employee Charlie Taylor to build a customised solution.

Taylor dutifully cracked open his tool box and created an engine which powered the Flyer's twin propellers by a sprocket chain drive. Sound familiar? Of course it does, it was basically a bigger and sturdier version of a bicycle chain. The Wright boys liked what they saw, fitted the engine and prepared for lift off.

The rest is aeronautical history but sadly from a two-wheeled perspective, the brothers soaring success inevitably turned their heads and they lost interest in the Wright Cycle Company. It closed down in 1909 but it's certainly worth reminding the modern Boeing Dreamliner or Airbus A380 of the debt they owe to the humble bicycle and its chain.

ANSWERING THE CALL OF NATURE
1893

Professional cycling isn't all about speed, power and fitness. Riders, of course, have to be fine physical specimens with thighs the size of tree trunks, but racing is also a battle of wits and planning. Tactics can make all the difference between the euphoria of success and the misery of failure, and those who innovate frequently prevail.

A leading early exponent of thinking outside the box was Charles Terront, arguably the first superstar of French cycling and a man who, as we shall see, was acutely aware that the mind is the body's most powerful muscle.

Terront's quick thinking was certainly in evidence in 1893 when he was invited to race against compatriot Valentin Corre in a 1,000km (621 mile) challenge staged at the Galerie des Machines in Paris. The two rivals were to go *mano-a-mano* – the first rider over the line takes all.

The race was certainly a marathon rather than a sprint but the two protagonists were evenly matched and as the hours slowly passed, there was little to choose between them. What could possibly separate the two gladiators of the saddle?

The pivotal moment came after 27 hours of pedalling when Corre finally accepted the inevitable, dismounted and hurried off for a long overdue 'comfort break'. Terront, however, ploughed on, and by the time Corre returned to the track, he found himself 2.5km (1½ miles) adrift.

Corre no doubt reasoned that he would make up the ground he had lost when Terront was forced to stop and pay his own visit *à la toilette* but the moment never materialised and three hours later it was Corre who once again was forced to pull over and dash to the urinals, losing yet more precious time. Answering the call of nature ultimately cost him the race as Terront completed the 1,000km (621 miles) in a time of 41 hours and 50 minutes, a comfortable 9.3km (5¾ miles) clear of his rival.

It was only when Corre's back-up team picked up the morning newspapers that they discovered Terront's secret courtesy of an eagle-eyed journalist, who revealed the winner did not in fact boast a bladder the size of a small swimming pool.

Terront had cut one of his inner tubes in half and tied a knot at one end. Whenever he felt the unmistakeable need to lighten the load, he would call over one of his support riders who would pull up alongside him and hand him the tube. Discreetly lowering it into his shorts, Terront would let nature takes its course and then merrily continue pedalling towards victory.

Corre had been comprehensively outwitted. 'Terront didn't even beat me by a tire,' he wryly told journalists after the race. 'He won by an inner tube.'

Terront won 54 major events during his 15-year career. He was twice crowned the French champion and also triumphed in the British national championship but in terms of sheer audacity, he never quite surpassed the cunning ruse he'd deployed in Paris.

ALL THAT GLITTERS
IS NOT GOLD
1896

The Olympics have produced some of British cycling's most magnificent and memorable moments in recent years but the nation's two-wheeled love affair with the Games began back in Athens in 1896 with the first Olympics of the modern era.

A modest 19 cyclists from just five countries were in Greece to compete in the six separate events, five of which were staged at the Neo Phaliron Velodrome while the road race was a 54-mile route from Athens to Marathon and back.

Britain sent a grand total of two riders, long-distance racer Edward Battel and endurance competitor Frederick Keeping, and both did us proud with Eddie coming third on the road and Freddy second in the 12-hour time trial.

The strange thing about the 1896 Games though was the fact the winning riders of the six inaugural races received silver rather than gold medals. The French team, who provided four of the six champions, were absolutely spitting.

The lack of gold medals was not a result of an economy drive by the Olympic organisers but rather a nod to the ancient Games in which winners were presented with an olive branch and hard currency rather than a shiny bauble around their necks.

The Athens organisers broke with tradition in commissioning artist Nicolas Gysis to design a silver and bronze medal for the 1896 Games for the winners and runners-up respectively but no gold medal. The medals featured a portrait of Zeus on one face and a representation of the Acropolis and the Parthenon on the other.

Gold medals for Olympic winners made their first appearance at the 1904 Games in St Louis, which was jolly good news for the

Americans who won all seven on offer in the cycling. A seemingly impressive feat until you realise that the States provided all 18 riders at the Games and no other country was represented.

Britain finally struck gold at the 1908 Olympics in London as Victor Johnson won over 603.5m (660 yards), Benjamin Jones triumphed in the 5000m (5500 yard) event, Clarence Kingsbury was the 20km (12½ mile) champion and Charles Bartlett was quickest over 100km (62 miles). And by the way, in 1908 eleven nations competed in the cycling event, unlike the previous Olympics. The gold rush was completed with victory in the team pursuit and Team GB departed *en masse* to celebrate their sensational success.

THE LAST MADISON SQUARE MARATHON
1898

A week may be a long time in politics but in America in the late 19th century, a mere six days must have felt like an absolute eternity for the riders who were brave or foolhardy enough to enter the Madison Square Garden 'six-day' event, a race so insanely gruelling that it should have come with a health warning, or at the very least some heavy sponsorship from a certain energy drink brand.

First staged in New York in 1891 the race, as the name suggests, was a straight endurance test staged over six consecutive days in which the competitors simply had to clock up as many miles as possible. Sleep was merely an optional extra and in theory the riders could pedal non-stop for the full six days. That's a potential 144 hours non-stop or 8640 minutes without a break.

The race initially proved hugely popular but as the competitors pushed themselves harder and harder, and suffered more and more, the sense of disquiet grew.

'It is a fine thing that a man astride two wheels can, in a six-day race, distance a hound, horse or a locomotive,' ran an editorial in the *New York Times* after the 1897 instalment of the race.

'It confirms the assumption, no longer much contested, that the human animal is superior to the other animals.

But this undisputed thing is being said in too solemn and painful a way at Madison Square Garden. An athletic contest in which participants 'go queer' in their heads, and strain their powers until their faces become hideous with the tortures that rack them, is not sport. It is brutality. Days and weeks of recuperation will be needed to put the Garden racers in condition, and it is likely that some of them will never recover from the strain.'

Things reached a head in 1898 when Charlie Miller was crowned champion. The American racked up a staggering 2088 miles in the six days of racing and spent just 15 hours off the track, sleeping for only nine and a half. However, so many of the other competitors were hospitalised with exhaustion that the authorities decided enough was enough and ruled that riders could in future only spend a maximum of 12 continuous hours in the saddle before they were required to rest.

The new edict, however, did not bring an end to endurance cycling. The teams quickly realised that by entering two riders, with each racing for 12 hours each, they could easily circumvent the restrictions and the modern Madison format – named in tribute to The Garden – was born.

And so 1898 was to be the last old-style race in New York but there is one fascinating footnote to the story, proving that while the physical demands of the event were far too much for some of the competitors, Miller at least was a fresh as a daisy.

It happened on the afternoon of the final day. Miller had established such a lead over his nearest rival that he could afford to abandon the track at 3.00pm. An hour-and-a-half later he remerged to get married to a young lady by the name Miss Hanson in front of the assembled spectators and after Miller had taken a victory lap of the track, the happy couple retired to the Waldorf-Astoria for their wedding night. It would, of course, be indelicate to speculate whether Mr and Mrs Miller had an early night or not.

NO PAIN NO GAIN
1904

It was Friedrich Nietzsche who said 'I assess the power of a will by how much resistance, pain, torture it endures and knows how to turn to its advantage.' The wily old German philosopher had clearly made the acquaintance of one or two professional racers.

Cycling has always been a tough gig. The agonising training is merely the hors d'oeuvres before the main event and in the melee of a frenetic race, accidents can and frequently do happen. Bikes get mangled and the riders often suffer much, much worse.

One of the most accident prone but durable cyclists of the professional era has to be Bobby Walthour, one of the first superstars of the burgeoning American cycling scene in the late 19th century and early 20th century and a man who redefined what it meant to pedal through the pain barrier.

Born in 1878, Walthour began his career as a sprinter but initially found fame riding in the gruelling and controversial 'six-day' format in the States (see The Last Madison Square Marathon, page 36), winning in New York in 1901 and again two years later.

It was, though, in the world of 'motor-pacing' – the once hugely popular format in which cyclists would race in the slipstream of a motorbike to achieve the highest speeds possible – that Walthour really hit the heights, winning the American Championship twice before heading to Europe in 1904 and sweeping all before him. In total he won 11 of the 12 races in which he rode was so dominant the French media slightly erroneously dubbed him 'L'Imbattable Walthour', 'The Unbeatable Walthour'.

But Motor-pacing was a dangerous endeavour and the litany of injuries Walthour suffered would surely have beaten a lesser man. During his career, he broke his left collarbone 18 times and his right 28 times. He accumulated a grand total of 115 stitches – 46 on his legs and 69 to his face and head – and he fractured his ribs 32 times. His eight broken fingers must have felt like little more than a minor inconvenience.

More seriously, he was twice pronounced dead at the scene after high-speed collisions with pace-setting motorbikes only to defy medical opinion, pick himself up and eventually return to the saddle.

Unbelievably Walthour was actually lucky in comparison to some of his motor-pacing contemporaries. Many died in the pursuit of even quicker times and it was undeniably a brutal way to go. Fellow America Harry Elkes was killed in front of 10,000 spectators in Boston when his rear tire exploded at 60mph while George Leander did not live to regret his bold assertion that 'only the clumsy get themselves killed' when he was thrown 5m (16½ft) into the air during a race in Paris. He fell onto the track, bounced into the seating and died in hospital 36 hours later.

Walthour mercifully continued racing until the 1920s but later life away from the track was not kind to him. 'His fortunes took a dramatic turn for the worse during World War I,' wrote Andrew Holman in his Walthour biography *Life In The Slipstream*. 'Most of his considerable wealth, which had been deposited in European banks, was confiscated by the Germans after the war broke out. Walthour's personal life also began to unravel. His marriage ended in divorce after his wife, who had become infatuated both with alcohol and another man while Walthour was away in France during the war, tried to kill him with a butcher knife.'

Motor-pacing, in comparison, probably came as a very welcome distraction.

THE TOUR'S EARLY TROUBLES
1904

Readers of a more mature vintage will remember the old British Rail slogan 'let the train take the strain'. Sadly too few commuters heeded the company's pithy, poetic invitation and dear old BR was privatised but the concept was essentially sound.

It proved a very bad idea, however, when Maurice Garin decided public transport rather than pedal power was the way forward during the 1904 Tour de France, an ill-advised move which saw the French rider stripped of the title and one of the most controversial Tours in history reach a dramatic and shameful denouement.

To describe the 1904 race, the second staging of the event, as mired in unseemly incident and general skullduggery would be an understatement. An understatement akin to dismissing Sir Chris Hoy's thighs as 'a bit big'.

From day one there was trouble. Garin and fellow French rider Lucien Pothier were ambushed and roughed up by four masked men, a competitor was disqualified for having 40 winks on the back seat of a car, another was caught slipstreaming behind another car and at one stage organisers had to fire shots into the air to disperse an angry crowd who had attacked the peloton in a bid to help local boy Antoine Fauré establish a lead. The mob did eventually disband but not before they'd knocked Italy's Giovanni Gerbi unconscious in the melée.

At other times, nails were also spread over parts of the course, rocks thrown at the cyclists and barricades erected. It was complete and utter madness.

It's easy, then, to imagine the feelings of sheer relief the organisers, let alone the riders must have initially felt when the anarchic tour finally came to an end in Paris on 23 July but the drama was far from over.

No sooner had Garin popped the champagne and posed for the mandatory pictures with the pretty girls who are always in attendance at such events, than the allegations of cheating began to pour in. Specifically, the winner was accused of taking the train during part of the race when he ought to have been in the saddle.

It may seem a preposterous allegation today. We live in a world of GPS, satellites and 24/7 live television coverage but back then riders were merely given route maps and told to register in each major town they passed through along the way. There were far fewer prying eyes to confute the cheats.

The Tour organisers really didn't want the bad publicity of an investigation but the Union Vélocipédique Française (UVF) stepped in, interviewed dozens of witnesses and eventually handed Garin a two-year ban for letting the train take the strain. The second, third and fourth-placed riders were also stripped of their finishes and fifth-placed Henri Cornet, a fresh-faced 19-year-old, was declared the winner.

For the record, Garin never admitted his guilt and the UVF paperwork connected to the investigation was subsequently lost during the First World War when it was hastily sent south as the Germans invaded, never to resurface again. A grand total of 29 riders were found guilty of a series of offences and the nascent event was on its knees.

'The Tour de France is finished and I'm afraid its second edition has been the last,' sobbed its founder Henri Desgrange. 'We have reached the end of the Tour and we are disgusted, frustrated and discouraged.'

Desgrange was, of course, wrong but it's impossible to stress how close the famous old race came to a premature and controversial end over a century ago.

THE TOUR'S MYSTERY MAN
1909

Since the first staging of the Tour de France back in 1903, thousands of riders have girded their loins, saddled up and accepted the legendary challenge of cycling's grandest and most gruelling Grand Tour event.

Some have found fame and fortune thanks to the Tour while others have struggled to make a significant impact. And then we have Georges Goffin, an elusive Belgian rider from the early 20th century who is arguably the worst competitor in the history of the Tour.

Details about Goffin's career are sketchy to the say the least. We do know he was born in Liege in French-speaking Belgium, he sometimes raced under the name of Georges Nemo and he first entered the Tour in 1904. In total he rode in five Tours but on each occasion he failed to even complete the first day's racing, a spectacular record of premature failure which no-one else has ever come close to emulating. No-one is quite sure exactly why the Belgian was unable to finish the first stage five separate times.

'The record of Belgium's Georges Goffin was one of persistent failure,' says *The Yellow Jersey Companion To The Tour de France*. 'Almost nothing is known about him, including why he rode under different names.'

Goffin, however, does not hold the record for the shortest ever Tour, a dubious distinction that goes to Englishmen Chris Boardman after he lasted a mere 90 seconds of the race in 1995.

In fact, Boardman didn't even ride in the Tour proper that year, crashing on a bend in Brittany during the Prologue stage of the event which resulted in an unscheduled trip to the local hospital.

'Storms flooded Brittany,' wrote French historian Jean-Paul Ollivier. 'The British rider came out of the start ramp like a rocket, took two or three bends at the very limit, a true acrobat, and went without limit through a wider bend. Propelled by his rare strength, his back wheel lifted into the air, hitting the barrier on the right of the road. [Team manager] Roger Legeay, who was following him by car, barely managed to miss him. Tally, several breaks to an ankle, cuts to his forearm, multiple bruises. Before it had even started, the Tour was finished without him.'

It took two hours of surgery to repair the damage to Boardman, which was exactly one hour, 58½ minutes longer than his race had lasted.

CHRISTOPHE BATTLES
THE ELEMENTS
1910

The 'Milan-San Remo' race is one of the five fabled 'Monuments' of European cycling, an acknowledged classic on the Continental racing calendar. At 298km (185 miles) long, it is also the longest one-day course on offer to professional riders and attracts hundreds of entrants and thousands of spectators in April every year.

First staged back in 1907, the race was originally organised by *La Gazzetta dello Sport* newspaper as a publicity stunt but it nearly came to a premature end in 1910 when unseasonably arctic conditions decimated the field and very nearly killed the eventual winner. The race's Italian nickname of *La Primavera* ('The Spring') presumably caught on much later.

Sixty-five intrepid competitors lined up for the start of the race on the freezing morning of 3 April. The average temperature for Milan at that time of year should have been a wonderfully comfortable 14°C but there was already snow on the ground and a bitter wind in the air.

Our brave winner was a Frenchman by the name of Eugenio Christophe, who finished the course in a time of 12½ hours, but it's no exaggeration to say he could have died on the way as he battled the elements. 'Not far from the summit I had to get off my bike because I started feeling bad,' Christophe recalled years later:

> 'My fingers were rigid, my feet numb, my legs stiff and I was shaking continuously. It was bleak and the wind made a low moaning noise
> 'In places there were 20cm (8in) of snow. Each time I was obliged to get off and push. Then I had to stop with

stomach cramp. I collapsed on to a rock at the side the road. I was freezing.

'I saw a house not far away but I couldn't get there. I didn't realise just what danger I was in. Happily in my misfortune a man chanced to pass by. I nodded towards the house and said *'casa'* [house] and he understood. He took me by the arm and led me to the house, which was a tiny inn.

'The landlord undressed me and wrapped me in a blanket. I murmured *'aqua caldo'* [hot water] and pointed at the bottles of rum. I did some physical exercises and I started to get some feeling back in my body.'

Unbelievably Christophe got back in the saddle to complete the race and collect the winner's cheque for 300 Francs but it took him a full month in hospital to recover from the frostbite he suffered and another two years before he regained full fitness.

The rest of the field did not fare any better. According to some reports only three other competitors made it to the finishing line but other accounts state that fourth-placed Cyrille van Hauwaert was disqualified for hanging onto the back of a car. If true, the Belgian should have been disqualified simply for not having the sense to get *inside* the motor.

DUBOC'S WATER
BOTTLE WOE
1911

Doping plagued the Tour de France for decades but it was the administration of different dubious substances that scandalised the 1911 instalment of the race when Paul Duboc was the victim of a Machiavellian poisoning which would have left even Sherlock Holmes bewildered and bemused.

The background to the Frenchman's unwilling intoxication goes something like this. Riding for the La Française-Diamant team, Duboc was beginning to make inroads into the advantage established by Tour leader Gustave Garrigou after winning stages eight and nine in the Pryenees and the race was alive with talk of Duboc pinching the lead from his compatriot.

The 327km (203 mile), tenth stage between Luchon and Bayonne was the ideal opportunity for him to maintain his momentum and after two hours hard riding, Duboc had left Garrigou in his wake and pressed on.

It was now time for the aforementioned poisoning incident. Duboc passed a watering station and grabbed a bottle. He pedalled on for a few more minutes but after quenching his thirst, he suddenly doubled up in pain and was unable to continue. Some unscrupulous bugger had nobbled his drink.

The race director Henri Desgrange later recalled rounding a bend in the road to see Duboc on the grass verge 'in a terrible state, struck with nausea that had turned him green, and suffering from terrible diarrhoea and painful vomiting. I smelled a bidon [water bottle] at his side and it didn't appear to me to have the odor of tea.'

Speculation about the identity of the poisoner was rife. Duboc's supporters pointed the finger at the Garrigou camp while others blamed a mysterious, disgruntled Tour rider with an axe to grind. *Les gendarmes* couldn't pin the Mickey Finn on anyone and the crime ultimately went unpunished.

To his credit, Duboc recovered sufficiently to pedal home 20 places behind Garrigou on the 10th stage and went on to win two more stages of the 1911 Tour. He eventually finished the race as runner-up to Garrigou but we'll never know whether he could have been crowned champion had it not been for his enforced and rather gruesome-sounding break.

Duboc earned another dubious claim to fame during the 1919 Tour when he broke a pedal axle. Desperate to repair the damage, he foolishly borrowed a car to find spare parts and was promptly disqualified by the race committee for cheating. Duboc protested his innocence but the organisers weren't budging.

THE PELISSIER PROTEST
1924

When we reluctantly turn our thoughts to the unedifying part doping has played in the history of the Tour de France and other events within professional cycling, we inevitably think of subterfuge, clandestine rendezvous with suppliers and, well, riders rather eager not to be exposed as cheats.

The 1924 Tour was startlingly different thanks to the Pelissier brothers – 1923 winner Henri and Francis – and what they revealed about what really went on behind-the-scenes during the famous race was as damning as it was ultimately unheeded.

The controversy was sparked by a heated row between Henri and race founder and organiser Henry Desgrange. A volatile and vocal man at the best of times, Henri was incandescent with rage after Desgrange would not allow him to remove one of his racing jerseys as the heat of the day took effect. It was a rule, albeit petty, that riders had to finish a stage with exactly the same clothing they began it in and Desgrange was not about to make any exceptions.

Henri had had enough. He quit the Tour, persuaded his brother Francis and fellow rider Maurice Ville to join his protest and then invited journalists to join them in the nearest café so he could vent at the iniquities of the Tour.

He initially limited his diatribe to lambasting Desgrange's rules and regulations but the talk then shifted to the excessive physical demands placed on the racers and how the riders coped with the miles and miles of racing.

'Do you want to see how we keep going?' Henri asked, reaching into a bag and producing a phial. 'That, that's cocaine for our eyes and chloroform for our gums.'

Ville tipped out the contents of his own bag to reveal boxes of mysterious pills. 'In short,' added Francis, 'we run on dynamite.'

The hacks hurried off to implore their editors to hold the front page but, in truth, the French public seemed more taken aback by the news of the withdrawal of their defending champion than his shocking revelations and amazingly Henri was allowed to ride the Tour again the following year.

He gave up cycling in 1927 but there was to be one more dramatic twist in what was a tumultuous life story. Henri's first wife Leonie committed suicide in 1933, shooting herself, and soon afterwards he began a relationship with Camille Tharault who was 20 years younger than him.

It was to prove a stormy liaison and in May 1935 it ended in further tragedy. After a bitter argument, Henri lunged at Camille with a knife at their villa outside Paris and cut her face. She fled to a bedroom where she found the same gun with which Leoni had killed herself two years earlier and confronted her lover. Henri lunged at her with the knife a second time and whether in genuine self defence or rage, Camille shot him five times.

'The tragic end of Henri Pelissier surprises no-one' reported the *Paris-Soir* newspaper. '"If I'd had the money I would have left him long ago" the murderess said yesterday.'

VICTOR DENIED VICTORY
1929

The relationship between a rider and his bicycle is essentially a simple one. The former provides the power and the latter bears the weight, and a cyclist really shouldn't be in the business of carrying his own bike around.

In the famous Tour de France of 1929 however that's exactly what happened to Victor Fontan, a heartbreaking example of terrible luck, mechanical malfunction and eventual failure which led to a major overhaul in the rules of the race.

It all happened on the 10th stage of the Tour, a mountainous and gruelling 323km (201 mile) stretch from Luchon to Perpignan. It was such a long route that the riders had set out before dawn to ensure they would finish the stage and as the race leader, Fontan proudly led them out wearing the Yellow Jersey.

He got less than 8km (five miles) before disaster struck. According to some reports he crashed into a gutter while others insist he collided with a dog but the end result was the same, his front forks were shattered and he needed another bike.

The problem was riders were not simply allowed to jump onto new wheels. They had to prove to the race judges that their bicycles were irreparably damaged and with the sun yet to rise on the 10th stage, there were no judges to be seen. Fontan had no second bike, no back-up team and, seemingly, no hope.

'Fontan was reduced to knocking on the doors of the villagers in the dark of the early morning looking for another bike that he might borrow,' relates Carol and Bill McGann in their book *The Story of the Tour de France*. 'At last he found a bike to resume the race, but he didn't just ride off. He couldn't. He had his broken bike strapped to his back. That year a rider had to finish with the bike he used to start the stage.'

For nearly 160km (100 miles), the Frenchman heroically pedalled on up and down the Pyrenees trying to catch the leaders with his mangled cycle weighing him down but it was mission impossible and he was eventually forced to quit.

He came to a halt in the village of Saint-Gaudens and began to cry as he realised his chance of Tour glory had disappeared. It was the first Tour to be covered by radio and Fontan's sobbing was recorded by two reporters and broadcast later the same day, sparking a national debate about the rule which had cost him so dearly.

'How can a man lose the Tour de France because of an accident to his bike? I can't understand it,' wrote the journalist Louis Delblat in *Les Echoes des Sports*. 'The rule should be changed so that a rider with no chance of winning can give his bike to his leader, or there should be a car with several spare bicycles. You lose the Tour de France when you find someone better than you are. You don't lose it through a stupid accident to your machine.'

The public mood was sympathetic and the following year the Tour organiser Henri Desgrange bowed to the pressure and legalised the use of replacement bikes as well as back-up teams, who could now help the riders with repairs. Fontan was back to compete again in the 1930 Tour as captain of the French team but his big chance had been the previous year and there was no fairytale return.

THE BIG BINDA BRIBE
1930

Everyone loves a champion. The thrill of witnessing a leading sportsman or woman at the very top of their game is a transcendent treat and those able to take their chosen game to a new level are artists indeed. Sport, after all, is about creating heroes.

The Italian rider Alfredo Binda should have been one of racing's undisputed heroes during his career in the 1920s and 1930s but while he was imperious out on the road, he eventually proved something of a turn-off with the cycling authorities. His talent was unquestionable but his popularity was not.

The problem was Binda was just *too* bloody good. 'Il Campionissimo' ('The Champion') won the Giro d'Italia for the first time in 1925 and returned in 1927 to dominate the race once again, winning 12 of the 15 stages en route to the title. He was champion again in 1928 and made it a hat-trick of triumphs a year later.

No-one could touch him and in recording three successive wins in the Giro, Binda won 33 of the total of 41 stages held. 'Cycling has always thrived off rivalry but Alfredo Binda never really had a proper rival,' explained John Foot in his book *Pedalare! Pedalare!* 'For much of his career he dominated the sport like a dictator (one of his nicknames) and his victories became so frequent that they almost became boring. A cult of personality developed around him, almost as if he were a god. He simply pulverised the opposition.'

The organisers of the Giro were getting fed up. The predictability of Binda's victories was beginning to impact on spectator numbers and the *Gazzetta dello Sport* newspaper wasn't shifting extra copies reporting yet another achievement by Alfredo.

Something had to be done, and after a clandestine meeting between Giro boss Emilio Colombo, Legano team owner Emilio Bozzi and other assorted men in suits, it was decided to offer the unbeatable Binda a cash incentive – aka a large bribe – not to ride in the 1930 race.

Binda reportedly agreed it might well be time to let someone else have a crack at the title and agreed to sit this one out. There was one condition and that was his pay-off had to equate to the same as he would have earned had he won the Giro once again, plus additional cash for his projected six stage wins, his Legnano team bonus plus other bits and bobs. The final bill, he insisted would be a whopping 22,500 lire. A smooth operator, our Alfredo.

Colombo and co were stunned. They'd budgeted for far less but they'd come this far and reluctantly agreed to his demands and the way was rather expensively paved for fellow Italian Luigi Marchisio to have his 15 minutes of fame.

Binda spent the summer of 1930 riding in the Tour de France. He won the eighth and nine stages of the race before pulling out, doubtless eager to leave enough time to spend his unexpected windfall on the French Riviera. He was though back on the winner's podium when he wrapped up a fifth Giro d'Italia title in 1933 as Colombo conceded he could no longer afford to keep Alfredo away.

OLYMPIC SKULLDUGGERY
1936

The men's 100km (62 mile) individual road race at the 1936 Olympics Games in Berlin was an absolute belter. A little less Nazi regalia draped around the Olympiastadion for the climax of the event would have been nice but the cycling itself was superb.

The race came down to a shootout between fellow Frenchmen Guy Lapebie and Robert Charpentier. Lapebie hit the front inside the stadium with 100m (330ft) to go but was dramatically overhauled by his compatriot just before the line. Charpentier claimed gold and Lapebie, just 0.2 agonising seconds behind his team-mate, had to settle for silver.

That would have been the end of that but the action had been captured by director Leni Riefenstahl, a Nazi propaganda film maker who was a big fan of Adolf Hitler. Despite her dubious political views, she was jolly handy with a camera. The result of Riefenstahl's efforts was the film *Olympia* and when it was released in France, Lapebie headed to his local cinema for a look. He nearly choked on his pop corn when he saw the final edit.

Riefenstahl had done a superb job in filming the final moments of the road race. Lapebie watched himself enter the Olympiastadion. He saw himself hit the front of the pack. He witnessed Charpentier counter attack and then, to his horror, he saw his rival tug at the back of his shorts moments before going past him to take gold.

Quelle horreur! Lapebie was incandescent and wasn't slow to let everyone know he now believed he had been the victim of skulduggery. 'I was tugged backwards at the last moment,' he raged. 'From the day I saw that film, I considered myself the moral victor of the Olympic Games.'

Strong stuff but Charpentier was in no mood to hold his hand up and swap medals. 'That is the biggest lie I have ever heard,' he responded. 'I'll sue Lapebie for defamation, even if it costs me a month's wages.'

Thanks to the wonder of modern technology and a well-known website that is replete with videos of kittens falling off washing machines, it's possible to see highlights of the contentious 1936 race but, sadly, it's inconclusive whether Charpentier was a massive cheat or Lapebie merely a bad loser.

The record books remain in the Charpentier camp while Lapebie did at least win gold in the team road race and team pursuit in 1936. And one of his team-mates in both those Olympic triumphs? Monsieur Robert Charpentier, of course.

WAR ON WHEELS
1937

When it comes to a spot of argy-bargy in a war zone, tanks are traditionally the go-to vehicle. Your average Panzer or Sherman is simply brimming with heavy armour, machine guns and cannons and relishes the prospect of venturing where angels fear to tread and having a dust-up. Bicycles ... not so much, but that has not precluded our two-wheeled friends from playing a major role in a series of historical conflicts.

The first recorded use of bikes in battle was in South Africa in 1896 during a minor skirmish known as the Jamieson Raid before the Second Boer War but it was the ominous advent of World War One that saw cycles pressed into active service for the first time on a large scale.

All the main protagonists deployed cycle-mounted infantry as well as scouts, messengers and even medical personnel on bikes but it was still the heavy artillery and (later in the war) tanks which held sway and the intrepid souls who pedalled into action were very much the supporting cast.

The first major role for bellicose bikes came during the Second Sino-Japanese War in 1937 when 50,000 Japanese troops swarmed into China *en masse* in the saddle. Like the Spanish Inquisition, the Chinese definitely weren't expecting that and the tactic proved hugely successful. So much so that the Japanese repeated the trick during the Second World War in the Malay Peninsula en route to capturing Singapore, using the speed of their free-wheeling soldiers through the jungle to outflank the retreating Allied Forces and generally cause mayhem.

During the Second World War the British employed airborne 'Cycle Commandos' who were issued with folding bikes, ordered to jump out of a plane and pedal off and bash the Bosch. The tactic was discontinued when the troops quite reasonably pointed out the sight of them unpacking their cycles tended to elicit giggles rather than fear from the German ranks.

In more recent years, the Viet Cong made good use of bicycles along the Ho Chi Minh Trail during the Vietnam War to transport supplies and avoid American napalm but the advent of laser-guided missiles, drone planes and even bigger, badder bombs has sadly seen the bike's effectiveness in battle wane.

The last country to boast a full-time regiment of bicycle-mounted troops was Switzerland but even they finally realised the folly of putting their national security in the hands of soldiers armed only with two wheels, puncture-repair kits and impossibly complicated pen knives.

'The Swiss have decided that pedal power has no place in plans to modernise and professionalise the army,' reported the BBC in 2001 when news broke that the military cyclists were for the chop.

'During the Second World War, the cyclists defended Switzerland's borders against the threat of Nazi attack.

'Only the fittest of the fit get into the cycling regiment. Recruits face a rigorous training regime which includes a 200km (124 mile) forced pedal march starting at two in the morning. The bikes weigh 25k (55lb) without luggage and at least twice that fully-laden with equipment including anti-tank weapons.

'But the government has decided that this unique brand of military service is no longer needed. In a new technologically-advanced army, there is no room for the unprotected pedal pushers.'

A YEAR IN
THE SADDLE
1939

Anglo-Australian sporting rivalry is a deadly serious business. The ongoing battle for supremacy between the old colonial power and the uncouth Antipodean upstarts, sorry, our proud Australian cousins, has defined both nations over the decades and the intensity of battle shows no signs of abating.

It was the same story in cycling in the 1930s with the two countries pedalling furiously for superiority in the saddle and one of the most hotly contested disciplines was the gruelling world of endurance riding, a format in which riders would attempt to clock up the most miles in a single calendar year. It was, frankly, insanity on two wheels.

The two main protagonists in this tale of self-inflicted torture and torment were Australia's Ossie Nicholson and England's Tommy Godwin and the tussle for national pride reached a head in 1937 when Nicholson set a phenomenal new record of 100,837km (62,657 miles) after 365 days on the road.

The Australian smugness was unbearable and on 1 January, 1939 Godwin set off at five o'clock in the morning in a bid to wrestle the record back for dear old Blighty. It was the start of a remarkable journey which saw him crisscross the country as he relentlessly piled on the miles.

Godwin (not to be confused with the Olympic cyclist Tommy Godwin who won bronze medals at the 1948 London Olympics) had bases in Stoke-On-Trent and Hemel Hempstead and he planned his daily routes to end at either one so that he could conveniently collapse and, hopefully, recover in time for the next day's challenge. His bike was a four speed, steel-framed mount supplied by his sponsors,

Raleigh, and although it may have been state-of-the-art for the era, it was a distinctly unwieldy and heavy piece of equipment compared to its modern successors.

His 'fuel' for his epic trial was nothing more than a modest diet of bread, milk, eggs and cheese. Godwin had become a vegetarian after briefly working in a pie-making factory as a teenager and he was also tee-total, ensuring he was never hungover when he embarked on yet another energy-sapping early-morning start.

Nicholson's record was within sight and on 26 October, Godwin surpassed the Australian's accumulated mileage when he rode triumphantly into London.

'He prepared himself on this Thursday morning October 26, for a gentle ride to Trafalgar Square and the planned reception,' wrote Godfrey Barlow in his book *Unsurpassed: The Story of Tommy Godwin, The World's Greatest Distance Cyclist*. 'The ride turned out to be far from gentle as it was cold, wet and sleet was falling, making conditions far from ideal. The weather reminded Tommy of the day he set out back in January, 299 days ago.'

A proud nation rejoiced, Tommy was granted an audience with the Prince of Wales and it all went very quiet Down Under.

He was not finished yet though. After taking the day off for his impromptu royal engagement, Godwin was back in the saddle and by the end of his day's riding on 31 December, he had clocked an incredible 120,805km (75,065 miles) in the year. That's a staggering average of 331km (205.65 miles) each and every day, the equivalent of cycling from London to Manchester. He spent an average of 18 hours each day riding and on 21 June recorded 581km (361 miles), his longest daily distance throughout the year.

No-one would now have begrudged Tommy a thoroughly-deserved rest but he was nothing if not determined and despite having put Nicholson firmly in his place, he ploughed on. And on and on. His new target was to set a new record for the fastest man to clock up 100,000 miles (1609,344km) and on 14 May, 500 days after setting off, he reached his milestone.

It was finally time for Tommy to get off the bike. He was so exhausted by his exertions that he reportedly complained of seeing pink elephants and it took him weeks to be able to walk properly.

His feat was recorded in the fabled *Golden Book Of Cycling* at the end of 1939 but his achievement no longer features in the *Guinness Book Of Records* because the editors believe it would be total and utter madness for anyone to attempt to eclipse Tommy's record. They've probably got a point.

THE BRAVERY OF BARTALI
1943

We have already learned how bicycles have been deployed as instruments of aggression in times of conflict (see War On Wheels, page 56) but they have also been a force for good during combat, proving the humble cycle can actually save lives.

The two-wheeled hero of our story is Gino Bartali. The Italian famously won the Giro d'Italia twice as well as the 1938 Tour de France before the outbreak of the Second World War the following year but whatever he achieved as a professional rider, he easily eclipsed with his fearless and selfless actions during the hostilities.

It was a terrible time for Italy's Jewish community. The formation of the Italian Social Republic in 1943, a puppet state controlled by Germany, saw the Jews persecuted and hunted by the Nazis and Italian fascists alike. Bartali did not like what he saw and decided to do something about it.

He made contact with the Italian and Jewish Resistance. Specifically, he began to courier forged travel documents to help Jews escape the country, riding out from his home in Florence every morning to collect photographs from those hiding in a local convent and with the pictures safely stashed in the frame of his bike, he'd return to the city and meet up with the forgers. The Italian police and the German troops were reluctant to search the celebrated cyclist despite stopping him daily at their checkpoints and under the pretence of training, Bartali was able to brazenly help thousands flee. According to a report by the Italian newspaper *Corriere della Sera* in 2003, some 800 Jews escaped as a direct result of his clandestine cycling.

He was eventually arrested by Mussolini's black shirts, taken to a villa infamous as a torture centre and ordered to stop his riding. 'I do what I feel,' he defiantly replied.

His heroics did not stop there, however, and when Nazi forces occupied Florence in 1943, he gave shelter to a displaced Jewish family in the cellar of his home in Via Del Bandino on the outskirts of the city, apparently dismissing the danger to himself and his own family had their guests been discovered by the Germans.

'The cellar was very small,' recalled Giorgio Goldenberg, one of the family saved by Bartali's bravery. 'A door gave way onto a courtyard, but I couldn't go out because that would run the risk of me being seen by the tenants of the nearby apartment buildings. The four of us slept on a double bed. My father never went out, while my mother often went out with two flasks to get water from some well.'

The arrival of the British army in August 1944 saw the Goldenberg's subterranean ordeal come to an end but it was not until 2010 that details of Bartali's actions emerged. The man was as modest as he was compassionate.

The end of the war saw Bartali return to professional cycling and he was soon back to his winning ways, triumphing at the 1946 Giro d'Italia before completing his second success at the Tour de France two years later. He died in 2000 at the age of 85, the end of a heroic and uplifting story which is a wonderful testament to both altruism and pedal power.

TOEING THE LINE
1947

It's no secret that riders of all eras have to make huge sacrifices to compete in the Tour de France. Racers put in countless hours of lonely training out on the roads and the agony of riding the Tour itself is legendary.

But few surely have made as big a sacrifice as the hapless French competitor Apo Lazarides, a man who took loyalty to a whole new level in 1947 when he received a rather onerous order from his team's lead rider.

The demanding 'grand fromage' in question was René Vietto, who had finished second in the 1939 Tour and was a notoriously fierce competitor and hardman. Potential disaster struck however during his preparations for the 1947 Tour when a toe became infected with sepsis and rather than miss the race, he ordered the doctor to amputate.

Vietto was, it seems, also a man who firmly believed in unity and after his operation he instructed Lazarides, his team 'domestique' or subordinate, to follow suit and get one of his own toes lopped off so that he might better understand the sacrifice required of Tour riders. He did as he was told and walked with a limp for the rest of his life as result.

Dear old Apo actually had previous when it came to erratic behaviour in the race. 'Apo was an unusually impressionable fellow,' wrote Tim Moore in his book *French Revolutions: Cycling the Tour de France*. 'The year before [1946], leading the peloton by a county mile up the Izoard, he was seized by an imminent fear of attack by wild bears and stopped to wait for the rest to catch up.'

For the record, the nine-toed Vietto finished fifth in 1947 while the dutiful Lazarides, ahem, limped home in a reasonably respectable tenth. Legend has it that the more ghoulish cycling fan can view Vietto's toe perfectly preserved in a jar of formaldehyde behind the bar in a café in Marseilles. The fate of Apo's perfectly healthy toe is unknown but it's unlikely he kept his discarded digit as a macbre memento of his painful Tour career.

CHICAGO DEFIES CONVENTION
1948

Almost as soon as the modern bicycle was born, forward-thinking enthusiasts armed with an alarming array of tools began to modify, adapt and generally pimp the classic design. Most of the mutated cycles that have resulted have served absolutely no practical purpose but the devil makes work for idle hands and it's an essentially harmless hobby.

The first golden era of bike pimping came in the wake of the Second World War in the United States as our cousins across the pond grew weary of riding mundane, conventional cycles and decided to get to work in their garages. The epicentre of the craze was Chicago and in true American style, what they produced was bigger and more bizarre than anything the cycling fraternity had seen before.

'To [the] Webster [dictionary] a bicycle is 'a light vehicle having two wheels, one behind the other',' read an article in the December 1948 issue of *Time* magazine.

'Such a definition theoretically describes the contraptions but fails to do justice to the imagination of the Chicago chapter of the National Bicycle Dealers' Association.

'By artfully applying welders' torches to metal tubing, the chapter's members transform ordinary, utilitarian bicycles into travelling monstrosities.

'By far the most outlandish ideas have come from the Steinlauf family, who produced from their bicycle-repair shop most of the oddities. They are hazardous, generally at least one member of the clan is to be found in the hospital.'

Some of their creations – black-and-white pictures of which can be found with a cursory search of the world wide web – were certainly something to behold. A bike with square wheels was only the beginning for the Chicago innovators. They adapted the traditional concept of the tandem so that the two riders sat side-by-side rather than one in front of the other and they also produced a five-seater bike. The bike with a series of metal spikes running on the outside of each wheel was even more surreal.

Their pièce de résistance, however, had to be what *Time* dubbed the 'Gangbuster Bike', a conventional tandem armed to the teeth with weapons. In total, it boasted 13 shotguns, two revolvers, six bayonets and even a flare gun – all mounted on the frame of the tandem – and in Chicago at least, must have gone a long way to redressing the traditional pre-eminence of cars on the local roads.

AT ONE WITH NATURE
1954

The theme of discarded and forgotten childhood toys is one entertainingly explored in the *Toy Story* films but sometimes real life is even more unbelievable than the big screen, as proven by the remarkable tale of Don Puz and his missing bicycle.

It was back in 1954 when the Puz family moved to Vashon Island in the state of Washington. Mrs Puz had been recently widowed and a generous member of the local community gave the family a children's cycle as a welcome present. It was a girl's bike but, Mrs Puz decided, it was exactly the right size for a then eight-year-old Don and the poor lad had to suffer the considerable indignity of riding it around town.

Unsurprisingly it was not long before Don 'lost' the bike and the family quickly forgot all about it.

Fast forward to 2012 and Mrs Puz, now 99-years-old, is reading the local newspaper and notices a story about an old bike that has been discovered behind a local restaurant. Nothing unusual there until she reads on and learns that the cycle has been 'eaten' by a tree and is 1.5m (5ft) in the air.

A puzzled Mrs Puz and Don headed down to the eaterie for a look and after closer inspection confirmed that the bike was indeed the one which Don had abandoned more than half a century ago. He had left it propped it up against the tree and over the intervening 58 years, the tree had grown up around the bike's frame, lifting it slowly but surely into the air as it matured.

It's an astonishing tale but the cherry on the cake was the revelation that the bike's front wheel, unencumbered by the trunk of the tree, still turned.

NOT A PRETTY PICTURE
1956

Britain's Olympic cycling adventure began in Athens back in 1896 (see All That Glitters is not Gold, page 34) and while the Games have rewarded us with plenty of thrills and spills, not to mention a flood of gold medals in recent years, British riders have not always enjoyed the best of luck at pivotal moments.

A desperately disappointing case in point occurred during the team road race at the 1956 Olympics in Melbourne and underlined the fine and frequently ridiculous line between success and failure.

The three-man British team for the race consisted of Alan Jackson, the appropriately named Arthur Brittain and 20-year-old Yorkshireman Billy Holmes and hopes were high our brave lads could become the Olympic champions.

Despite the searing temperature Down Under, everything was going according to plan until the 120km (75 mile) point of the 188km (117 mile) race when young Holmes slowed down to grab a wet sponge from one of the race helpers and an over-eager photographer suddenly jumped into the road to take his picture. Billy never saw him coming and rider and idiotic snapper collided.

A few bumps and bruises weren't going to slow Billy down but his badly buckled front wheel inevitably did and it took minutes to find a replacement. He lost valuable time on the leaders and at the end of the race, he limped over the line in 14th place.

Jackson came third and Brittain sixth, and had Holmes been able to come in 12th or better, they would have edged out the French for gold. As it was they had to settle for silver and Billy was last spotted clutching a bicycle pump, whispering darkly about finding the offending snapper.

The whole race was a bit of a farce and the start was delayed when three Irish riders hijacked proceedings. The trio of Irish Nationalists were not even supposed to be in Melbourne because they were members of the National Cycling Association of Ireland, a body not recognised by the International Cycling Union, but they somehow managed to conceal themselves among the field of 88 legitimate riders before causing chaos by shouting Nationalist slogans and handing out pamphlets. The Aussie boys in blue were called and the ill-fated race could not start before the three protestors were hauled off in handcuffs.

The controversy did not end there and there were squeals of protest from both Britain and France after Italian rider Ercole Baldini crossed the finishing line first, both teams claiming he had deliberately ridden the final stages of the race sandwiched between two film trucks to unfairly shield himself from the wind. The complaints were dismissed but the sense of anger either side of the Channel was, at best, thinly disguised.

To cap a thoroughly chaotic day, the tape recorder with the national anthems failed to work during the medal presentation ceremony and Team GB left in silence, vowing to run over the next photographer stupid enough to cross their path.

UNBEATABLE BERYL
1959

The exhilarating exploits of Victoria Pendleton, Lizzie Armitstead, Emma Pooley, Nicole Cooke *et al* in recent years has seen the profile of women's cycling in Britain rise to unprecedented, dizzy heights. The fairer sex have been looking sharper in the saddle than the heels on a pair of Manolo Blahniks lately.

The godmother of women's cycling in Blighty, however, has to be the late, great Beryl Burton, a lady who redefined the meaning of sporting domination and whose longevity would make the Duracell bunny blush.

Born in Leeds in 1937, she was introduced to the joys of cycling by her husband Charlie and in 1957 she won silver at the national individual time-trial championship. It was to prove merely the beginning of truly phenomenal career.

Our Beryl proceeded to wipe the floor with the opposition. 'No other British sportswoman has dominated their field in the way that Beryl Burton dominated the world of cycling,' read her obituary in *The Independent* following her death in 1996. 'As *Velo Gotha*, the Belgian bible of cycling facts and figures succinctly puts it: 'She was the best known and most successful woman cyclist'. In the course of a career that spanned five decades, the fiercely competitive Yorkshirewoman won seven world titles – two road race championships and five track pursuit titles, and 96 national titles – 12 road race championships, 13 pursuit titles and 71 time trial titles against the clock.'

These considerable achievements though were only the tip of the iceberg and Beryl is perhaps best and most fondly remembered for two iconic feats.

The first occurred in 1967 when she set a new national record of 446km (277.25 miles) in a 12-hour time trial. That in itself would have been impressive enough but in setting the record Beryl overtook Mike McNamara – who was in the process of setting the men's 12-hour record – and according to legend impudently offered Mike a liquorice allsort which he sheepishly accepted. For two years, Beryl's 446km (277 mile) mark was a record for any British cyclist, male or female.

Her other great claim to fame was her remarkable record in, deep breath now, the Road Time Trials Council's British Best All-Rounder competition, a convoluted way of describing the process of finding the best overall rider in the country.

Beryl was first crowned champion in 1959 and for 25 consecutive years she remained unbeaten and unbowed, claiming her last title in 1984. That's an unblemished quarter of a century as champion. It's also worth noting Beryl was an amateur, a proud housewife and occasional fruit picker and worker in the rhubarb farms in Yorkshire and training and competing had to be balanced with family life.

She died young, at the age of just 58, but she left an indelible mark on her beloved sport. Awarded an MBE in 1964 and made an OBE four years later, her life was celebrated in 2012 in a Radio 4 play entitled *Beryl: a Love Story on Two Wheels*, an epitaph which says it all.

AU REVOIR, MONSIEUR LE PRESIDENT
1960

Etiquette can be a problematic convention. One man's due deference can be another man's discourtesy and unless someone explains the rules, it's remarkably easy for protocol to fall victim to confusion and ignorance.

And so it was on the penultimate stage of the 1960 Tour de France from Besançon to Troyes when the organisers unexpectedly learned that a rather important spectator would be watching the race. The VIP in question was none less than the French President, General de Gaulle who, they were told, would be at the bottom of his garden in the village of Colombey-les-Deux-Eglises near Troyes to cheer the peloton through.

The Tour director Jacques Goddet hit on the idea of an impromptu tribute to the hugely popular President and quickly located French national champion Henry Anglade to discuss his thoughts on the hoof.

'We were right at the end of the tour, the day before we finished in Paris,' Anglade recalled. 'I was at the back of the bunch when Jacques Goddet came up alongside me. He said "We've just learned that General de Gaulle is at Colombey. Would it be an inconvenience if the race stopped to greet him?" I said to him "You're asking all the riders to stop in full flight?"'

The experienced Anglade realised the dangers of the peloton coming to a dangerously abrupt halt en masse and began to forewarn his fellow competitors what was about to happen.

'I went back up to the head of the race to talk to the team leaders and then I dropped back down the bunch telling the other riders as they passed,' he said. 'Finally I dropped back to the race director's car to say that the riders had all agreed.'

The race entered Colombey at a sedate pace and then ground to an even more sedate stop outside de Gaulle's garden without destroying a single petunia. Pleasantries between some of the peloton's leading lights and the President were exchanged and Goddet's PR stunt appeared to have worked a treat.

That was until Frenchman Pierre Beuffeuil finally reached Colombey. The Centre-Midi team rider saw his dismounted rivals by the side of the road but rather than join them, he pedalled furiously onwards to Troyes. The peloton were absolutely flabbergasted but despite their frantic chase, they could not catch Beuffeuil and he claimed a shock stage victory.

The sting in the tail is it was not Beuffeuils' fault. He had suffered a puncture earlier in the stage and had spent most of the day playing catch-up. The message about the collective pause in proceedings had never reached him and he was certainly non the wiser when he suddenly came across his fellow riders taking time off.

Goddet wanted Beuffeuil charged with treason but when it was pointed out France was a republic rather than a constitutional monarchy, he knew he'd never make it stick.

CYCLING ON THE CURRICULUM
1961

In dear old Blighty, learning to ride safely used to be taught in school via the medium of the Cycling Proficiency Test. Introduced in October 1947, the CPT essentially involved swerving around a few judiciously placed obstacles in the playground and if you managed not to fall off, run over the tester's toes or maim the school guinea pig, you tended to pass.

The CPT has been replaced by the irritatingly modern 'Bikeability' scheme but the theory remains essentially the same. If you can get from A to B on two wheels with the minimum number of civilian casualties en route, you're in.

In the States, of course, they do things differently and when the St Helens School in Ohio was opened in 1961, the new headmaster decided unicycling would become a mandatory subject, reasoning it would be an engaging way to encourage physical education. The pupils were supplied with bikes and the school began to forge itself a bizarre reputation as the seat of learning of choice for those who liked pedalling on one wheel.

It was not long, however, before the unusual curriculum choice began to help swell the school's coffers. 'Unicycles have become the rage and trademark of one school, St Helen Parish School in Newbury, Ohio,' reported *The Tuscaloosa News* in an article in September 1970. 'Cycles are ridden by all of its 97 pupils. They're famous and their prowess has proven a profitable thing for the school. Teams of the best riders have been guests in Macy's parade and on national television variety shows and the school has won a contract from Goodyear to test the company's bike tyres.'

They also performed at the Inaugural Parade for Jimmy Carter as president in 1977, the Rose Bowl and World's Fair and it was not long before anxious, prospective parents were actually paying to have their kids privately tutored in the art of unicycling to ensure they got into the school.

Sadly, the appetite for the school's unique sporting activity slowly waned and by the early 1990s, unicycling in the corridors was no more. There was, though, a 2013 reunion for the alumni of 1965 to 1985 as past pupils pedalled their way down memory lane.

THE IDIOCY OF INERTIA
1965

He was a very clever man, Albert Einstein. The Nobel Prize winner's revolutionary theory of relativity remains one of the two central pillars of modern physics, his $E = mc^2$ formula is one of the famous in the world and he could finish *The Times* sudoku without breaking sweat.

He also knew a thing or two about bikes. 'Life is like riding a bicycle,' he wrote in a letter to his 20-year-old son Eduard in 1930. 'To keep your balance you must keep moving.' Wise words from Albert there but advice that Japanese Tsugunobu Mitsuishi decided to completely disregard when he set out to break one of cycling's most pointless records imaginable.

The nature of Mitsuishi's challenge? To remain completely stationary on a cycle without falling off for as long as possible. No pedalling, no forward motion, no tippy toes on the floor – just balancing on an untethered bike without keeling over.

The 39-year-old Tokyo man embarked on his quest back in 1965 and ignoring the heated debate about whether deliberately remaining motionless wasn't rather against the spirit of cycling, he managed to stay upright for a remarkable five hours and 25 minutes straight. Mitsuishi may have been a nutter but you've got to admire his poise.

Mercifully, his magnificent immobility appears to have discouraged anyone from attempting to surpass his milestone. There are no records of further, legitimate challenges to his bizarre record but further research does reveal there was one unnamed lady who thought she'd have a half-hearted shot at the title.

Sadly she didn't quite get to grips with the basic rules of the game, as *Guinness Book Of Records* co-founder Ross McWhirter revealed in an interview 10 years after Mitsuishi's soporific feat.

'There was a woman who demanded to be put in the book because she had sat on a stationary bicycle longer than anyone,' McWhirter explained. 'It turned out she had gone to a bicycle shop and sat on a bicycle with clamps and so on to hold it up. Whereas Tsugunobu Mitsuishi had balanced on a *real* bicycle. So I said to her, after all, you have to compare like with like. And she still kept writing letters.'

For anyone else contemplating an attempt to eclipse Mitsuishi's surreal achievement, exercise bikes don't count either.

THE WHITE
BIKE MAN
1965

You can barely move for 'Boris Bikes' in London these days. At the last count there were 8,000 of them in the capital and although the city has not yet become the Mecca for pedestrians and cyclists alike that some envisaged since the scheme's introduction in the summer of 2010, motorists can definitely detect the wind of change.

Unsurprisingly there's been a bit of a barney about who takes credit for the aforementioned sharing scheme. The rent-on-the-spot idea came to fruition during Boris Johnson's first term as London Mayor but it was his predecessor, Ken Livingstone, who originally floated the big idea back in 2008. The two politicians have been bickering over who gets the credit like squabbling schoolboys ever since.

The real mastermind behind the scheme, however, has to be the fabulously-named Laurens Maria Hendrikus Schimmelpennink, or Luud Schimmelpennink if you can't quite get your tongue round his full title, who pioneered the concept of free city cycling over in Holland in the 1960s.

Clever Luud was a member of the Provo group in Amsterdam, a free-thinking, radical group whose mission statement was to shake things up a bit. In July 1965 they published a pamphlet entitled *Provocation No.5* in which they advocated the use of free bikes to alleviate Amsterdam's congestion and pollution problems.

As usual, the Establishment was too busy enjoying their G&Ts and going to the opera to actually do anything, so Schimmelpennink and his chums assembled 10 or so bikes, painted them all white and simply left them around the city for anyone to use whenever they fancied. The embryonic 'White Bicycle Plan' was born.

Unfortunately, the long arm of the law was not happy and they ruled that leaving an unlocked bike on the streets of the capital was an offence. They heartlessly confiscated the lot.

'The plan was to stop the car, the destruction of the town, the pollution, by leaving cars outside the town and give a new instrument for people to use when they want to travel around,' Schimmelpennink explained in a recent interview.

> 'Free bikes, for everybody. But the police took them away, of course, in their feeling it was not allowed to put a bike without lock. The point was we were not making a system at that moment, we were making an idea.
>
> 'In the minds of the politicians, bikes were a thing of the past. In their opinion, the future was through the car. But they were wrong. We know that now in this moment, bikes are the future, and the car will be changed. It was a very powerful idea.'

Schimmelpennink was not beaten yet and adhered to the old mantra 'if you can't beat them, join them', winning election to the Municipal Council of the City of Amsterdam in early 1967 with the ambition of making the 'White Bicycle Plan' a reality.

He proposed flooding the city with 10,000 publicly funded bikes and although his ambitions plan was blocked by political opponents, you cannot kill an idea, and after a long period of germination, community bicycle schemes began to emerge in cities throughout Europe and North America.

Unlike Boris Johnson in London, Schimmelpennink never saw his name colloquially attached to the Amsterdam initiative, which was probably for the best in the interests of brevity.

OUT OF THIS WORLD
1973

According to Captain James T Kirk in *Star Trek*, his mission was 'to boldly go where no man has gone before.' It was a brave attitude which got him and his Federation chums on the *Enterprise* into a few tight corners – not least the sacrificial lamb who invariably got killed when they beamed down onto an alien planet each week – but you've still got to admire his sense of adventure.

It was exactly this real-life pioneering spirit that was the catalyst for the American Moon landings and, in due course, resulted in the first ever bicycle ride in space. Beat that, William Shatner.

The watershed moment came in 1973 during the Skylab 3 mission to the first American space station, Skylab. Three astronauts blasted off from the Kennedy Space Centre in Florida and once they'd successfully docked with the station, they began a series of medical experiments.

The commander of the mission was Alan Bean and although he already held the distinction as the fourth man to walk on the moon after flying on the Apollo 12 mission four years earlier, far greater fame beckoned when he became the first man to jump into the saddle outside the Earth's atmosphere.

To be clear, Bean did not actually disengage the air locks, pop on a suit and pedal out into the cold, dark abyss that is space. He was safely seated on a stationary bike inside the station, hooked up to all manner of gadgets and computers, and spent 90 minutes or so pedalling away to assess how he coped physically in the unique, gravity-free conditions. Bean, however, did have a novel way of timing his ride, eschewing his watch and instead pedalling for the time it took Skylab to make a complete orbit of the Earth.

BMX GETS A 'BUM' DEAL
1974

For some snooty cycling purists, BMX will forever be regarded as the black sheep of the two-wheeled family. To them it's an unruly and unkempt cousin that's just too loud and too brash for polite society. For everyone else, it's an absolute riot.

The stuffy traditionalists' attempts to give bicycle motocross the cold shoulder suffered a major blow in 2008 when it made its Olympic debut at the Beijing Games. The long fight for recognition and legitimacy was over and BMX had finally been accepted by its peers.

That battle for equal billing began in the States in 1970 when Scot Breithaupt, the undisputed godfather of BMX, organised the first ever 'official' race on a dirt track in California. The popularity of the sport exploded almost overnight and Breithaupt had a phenomenon on his hands.

There was, though, one minor fly in the ointment – Breithaupt decided to call his burgeoning new set-up the Bicycle United Motocross Society. That's B.U.M.S to you and me.

'I used to race motorcross and when I practiced local kids would come out and imitate my jumps,' Breithaupt explained. 'The original BMX track was 'B.U.M.S I' in Long Beach in California. It was gnarly. It was a trail that I used for practice on my motorcycle. I rode for the Yamaha factory as a support rider. The track was about 411m (450 yards) long and we ran two laps. It had a 10.7m (35ft) high drop-away jump, a mud hole and eight or nine other jumps.'

Despite its ridiculous acronym, the new umbrella group for BMXers flourished in the early 1970s and Breithaupt was organising bigger and bolder events.

'By 1974 I promoted the Yamaha Bicycle Gold Cup Series and had over 1000 riders at each event,' he said. 'We held the finals in the LA Coliseum. About 16,000 spectators were there, which is probably the biggest event ever to this day. It was huge.'

Exactly a decade later the same venue staged the opening ceremony of the Los Angeles Olympics and although it was to a further 24 years before a BMX was pedalled at the Games in Beijing, bicycle motocross was by then firmly on its way to getting a proper job, a sensible haircut and pension plan.

LUCK OF THE IRISH RUNS OUT
1975

Politics and sport have rarely made for happy bedfellows but the sporting boycott of South Africa during the Apartheid era was an exception to the rule, a powerful statement of intent to the country's white rulers that world would no longer tolerate their racist regime.

There were sanctions for those sportsmen and women who chose to ignore the boycott and the threat of suspension or a long ban led to all sorts of clandestine incidents as those who did travel to South Africa to compete went to great lengths to remain anonymous.

One such tale involved the Irish riders Pat McQuaid, who had recently won the Tour of Ireland, and Sean Kelly, the national junior champion, who accepted an invitation to compete in the 1975 instalment of the Rapport Tour between Cape Town and Johannesburg. Cycling's world body the Union Cycliste Internationale (UCI) had turned its back on South Africa five years earlier and both men knew they'd be in hot water indeed if details of their trip were to be made public.

They made it to South Africa undetected and racing under false names, it seemed they'd get away with it. That was until Elizabeth Taylor and Richard Burton unexpectedly made an appearance.

The famed Hollywood couple had just tied the knot for the second time and as part of their honeymoon, they arrived in Oudtshoom in the Western Cape for a stopover at exactly the same time McQuaid and Kelly and Rapport Tour were also in town.

A local reporter noticed there was 'British' team listed as taking part in the race and asked the manager whether he could organise a publicity picture with his riders and Taylor and Burton. The wheels were about to come off McQuaid and Kelly's subterfuge.

The team manager tried to pull the wool over the reporter's eyes by putting up a selection of local riders in place of the Irish boys but the ruse failed to throw him off the scent and after a bit of digging, he discovered the true identities of the racers.

'The secret team who masquerade as Britain,' ran the headline after the journalist sold the story to *The Daily Mail* and McQuaid and Kelly suddenly found themselves exposed.

The UCI were not amused and both men were banned for six months. Worse was to follow though when the UCI forwarded their names to the International Olympic Committee, who imposed lifetime bans on both and dashed their dreams of riding at the 1976 Games at Montreal.

Taylor and Burton divorced for a second time in 1976, presumably blissfully unaware of the impact their short lived marriage had had on Irish cycling.

The controversy, though, clearly didn't ruin McQuaid's long-term prospects, rising through the ranks as he did to become the president of the UCI in 2006, a perplexing example of the poacher becoming the extremely well remunerated gamekeeper.

THE BREAKAWAY THAT BACKFIRED
1978

There's an old saying that 'some rules are meant to be broken' but when it comes to the Tour de France, some unwritten rules are definitely sacrosanct. In particular, the convention that states that the peloton is a democracy rather than a free-for-all. The consequences for ignoring this can be severe, as naive French rider Dante Coccolo found to his cost during the 1978 Tour.

The incident occurred on a gruelling 209km (130 mile) stage from Bordeaux to Biarritz. It was a hot day, the 100-strong field had been taking on plenty of liquids and it was not long before some of the riders felt the inevitable call of nature. The collective cry for a comfort break went up and 30 or so competitors dashed behind the nearest bush.

The rest of the peloton did the decent thing and slowed down. All, that is, except for Coccolo, who cheekily decided to speed up and try to build a significant, if ill-gotten lead. It was a flagrant breach of protocol and a move he would quickly come to regret.

'He had a habit of attacking on bathroom breaks,' explained Paul Sherwen, a British rider who was in the *peloton* that day. 'He thought it was quite amusing. It's not illegal but if 20 or 30 guys stop for a break and you go off on an attack, you're going to make 20 or 30 enemies.'

'When it was Coccolo's turn for his own bathroom break and he put his bike down on the grass verge, a couple of guys slowed down and grabbed the bike. They wheeled it down the road for a kilometre or two and tossed it into a ditch. Everyone in the peloton was very happy about it.'

The dastardly Coccolo was now stranded and had to wait for five minutes before his Jobo-Spidel team car arrived to take him to locate his missing bike. He had to ride on the bonnet of the car, an ignominious end to a less than edifying day. The conniving Frenchman went on finish second last in that year's Tour and never competed in the race again. He was not sorely missed by his fellow riders.

HOY'S DEBT TO HOLLYWOOD
1982

It was definitely a mixed year at the movies back in 1982. On the one hand, cinemagoers were able to feast their eyes on cult classics *Blade Runner* and *Tron*, the epic *Ghandi* and acclaimed romantic drama *An Officer and a Gentleman*. On the other hand they could, if they were injudicious in their ticket purchases, find themselves subjected to *Porky's*, *The Thing* or *The Slumber Party Massacre*. If they were really unlucky, they might have even had to sit through *Annie*.

The most successful film of the year however was Steven Spielberg blockbuster *ET: The Extra-Terrestrial*, the touching tale of a young boy who befriends an alien stranded on Earth. It was a film that made Spielberg millions and irritatingly ensured the phrase 'phone home' was never far from every wag's lips.

More pertinently considering the theme of this book, it was also the movie directly responsible for Great Britain winning six Olympic cycling medals. For it was back in 1982 that a fresh-faced primary school kid from Edinburgh persuaded his dad to take him to the pictures to watch the film and British cycling would never be the same again. The young chap, of course, was Chris Hoy.

'I was watching *ET* when I was about six years of age and I'd never seen a BMX bike before,' Hoy admitted in 2013 when he announced his retirement. 'It's the scene at the end of the film when they're getting chased by the police. I just thought, wow, I'd like to give that a go. The BMX scenes were fantastic, so I pestered my dad into taking me along to the local track at Danderhall where I saw all these kids having terrific fun. That was it. I was hooked and it all sort of spiralled from there.'

The rest, as they say, is history. Hoy won his first gold at the Athens Olympics in 2004 in the 1km (1000 yard) time trial, a wonderful hat-trick of titles at the Games in Beijing and, finally, gold in both the Team Sprint and Keirin at the Velodrome at the 2012 Olympic Games in London in the climax to a glittering career.

Spielberg did rather well too after *ET* but while Hoy's career was without blemish, the American did blot his copybook when he produced *An American Tail: Fievel Goes West* in 1991 and directed *The Adventures of Tintin* twenty years later. Celluloid crimes for which we can probably forgive him after inspiring the most successful Olympian British cycling has ever produced.

MORGAN'S BEASTLY LEAP
1982

They say elephants never forget. It's never been made entirely clear why we imbue the big fellas with such good memories but it's probably safe to assume the nine African bull elephants who were corralled in a car park in Illinois back in 1982 never forget their unusual day out.

Circus elephants, of course, are no strangers to showbiz but our nine intrepid beasts had never seen anything like it as John 'Mercury' Morgan proceeded to successfully jump over all of them on a bright yellow bicycle. The stunt was part of a short lived American TV show called *That's Incredible!* and Morgan's nine-animal feat, a leap of some 15.25m (50ft), remains a world record for a bike jumping over elephants. Admittedly, it's not the most hotly contested of categories in the *Guinness Book Of World Records* but it's easy to mock.

Morgan's fascinating career as a stunt rider began in the 1970s when his mum refused to buy him a motorbike and his dreams of emulating Evel Knievel were cruelly dashed. It was pedal power or nothing for him and after practising flying over rubbish bins on his bike, he graduated up to leaping over cars and jumping through rings of fire. You know, the usual stuff.

The elephant stunt was inspired by his love of the circus and once he'd persuaded the producers of *That's Incredible!* that it would make great television, he got the green light. You can still watch footage of the jump on the web, although you are forewarned that his yellow jump suit isn't exactly easy on the eye and there is the small fact he needs a tow from a motorbike to reach the required speed to make the leap and avoid leaving tyre marks on the back of a disgruntled 15,000lb animal.

A few years later, Morgan fulfilled his dream of working in the circus when he was taken on by The Ringling Bros. and Barnam & Bailey outfit. The angry and suspicious looks from the circus' elephants on his first day told their own story.

INTO THE VALLEY OF DEATH
1983

According to Alfred, Lord Tennyson's famous Crimean War poem *The Charge of the Light Brigade*, it was the six hundred who recklessly rode 'into the valley of Death.' To be fair, they were only obeying orders but only half of them made it back in one piece and it wasn't the smartest move ever.

The two-wheeled equivalent of the infamous British charge must surely be the Furnace Creek 508 race in America. For Valley of Death read the Death Valley desert, for 600 cavalry read 250 cyclists and for insanely ill-advised read, well, insanely ill-advised.

First staged in 1983, the Furnace Creek 508 bills itself as the 'toughest 48 hours in sport' and when you take a closer look at the route riders must follow to complete the gruelling 817.5km (508 mile) race, it's very hard to disagree.

Competitors begin in the salubrious surroundings of Santa Clarita, 40km (25 miles) north of Los Angeles, and must pedal across Death Valley before finishing in the marvellously named town of Twentynine Palms. The halfway point takes the cyclists through Furnace Creek in the desert (hence the name) where, fact fans, a staggering record air temperature of 56.7°C was recorded back in 1913. Which is seriously hot.

Riders have 48 hours to complete the crazy course – first across the lines wins – but if the desert and the extreme heat weren't enough to contend with, the route is also far from flat. In fact, it rises and falls so dramatically that completing the 508 means competitors are riding the equivalent of four mountain stages of the Tour de France back-to-back.

Unsurprisingly, only about 60 per cent of entrants in the individual race actually complete the course but mercifully for them, unlike the poor sods in the Charge of the Light Brigade, they simply retire from the race rather than get blown to pieces by Russian cannons.

A brutal event the 508, then, but it does boast one endearing, rather cuddly feature. Competitors in the race are not identified by numbers but rather by 'totems', animal-based nicknames which they can choose themselves or are assigned by the organisers.

Past individual and relay competitors have gone for totems such as 'Chesapeake Bay Retriever', 'Raven Lunatics', 'Relucent Phoenix' and 'Pudu and the Pussycats' but the award for the least confidence inspiring choice has to go to the rider who elected to be called the 'Banana Slug'.

THE GLOBAL DASH
1984

It was dear old Thomas Stevens (see The Amazing Travels of Thomas, page 22) who first contemplated the insanity that is pedalling around the world, and ever since his successful circumnavigation was completed back in 1887, deranged riders and cracked cyclists have been following faithfully in his tyre tracks.

It took Thomas two years and nine months to complete his remarkable journey. To be fair, he enjoyed some extremely generous and leisurely stopovers along the way, but back then simply getting from A to B (and eventually all the way back to A again) rather than sheer speed was the main priority.

Ever since 1984, however, his spiritual successors have been all about the pace as they've battled for the coveted title of the *Guinness World Records* (GWR) fastest circumnavigation of the globe, a challenge so ridiculously arduous that it really should come with a health warning, a big scary skull and crossbones and 'Police Line Do Not Cross' tape.

The first to set a time was Brit Nick Sanders in 1984, who pedalled a 20,921km (13,000 mile) route across the northern hemisphere in 78 days. His verified record stood until 2003 when GWR suddenly changed the rules to require challengers to cover 40,073km (24,900 miles), including the unavoidable ocean crossings by air or boat, via two antipodal points and rather harshly, Sanders' efforts were summarily expunged from the record books.

Since then, many have tried and most have failed to set a new milestone but Mike Hall was successful in 2012 when he set off from the Royal Observatory in Greenwich in June, returning to the same spot a staggering 91 days and 18 hours later.

Hall averaged roughly 322km (200 miles) a day on a journey which took him through 20 countries and four continents and it was patently obvious when he arrived back in London that the trip had nearly beaten him.

'I think I had a lot of the emotions in the last few weeks on the roads,' he said after crossing the finishing line. 'It was quite difficult and I think it builds up, the stress. So I kind of released all that in the last few days.

'There's been some moments, some kind of breakdowns, but I keep the breakdowns on the bike. I don't stop for those. I broke my bike [in Albania] but managed to fix it with some parts I had, then had to ride through the night to get to Greece. There were a few close calls with traffic but I just tried to keep safe, keep vigilant.'

Hall's fragile mood did not improve a few weeks later. In their infinite wisdom, the good people at GWR decided to change the record criteria once again and decreed that the time spent in the air or on the sea had to be added to the time actually spent in the saddle and Hall's journey time was recalculated to 107 days, two hours and 30 minutes.

This meant that, thanks to all the tinkering with the rules and regulations, the current certified record still belongs to British cyclist Alan Bate who in August 2010 completed the feat in 106 days 10 hours and 33 minutes.

'LOOK, NO HANDS!'
1985

For many cyclists, true happiness is simply finding the right stretch of road on which to pedal. Whether it's a stunning coastal route, a picturesque rural B-road or a woodland path through the flora and fauna, cycling is an experience which can be significantly enhanced by the right surroundings.

Mountainous routes also tend to be popular despite the exertion required to get to the top. The panoramic views, the invariably twisting tarmac and the sense of sheer escape can make an elevated road irresistible. If you live in the hills, you've got no choice anyway.

One of the most spectacular mountain routes in the world is the breathtaking Stelvio Pass in Italy. It lies in the Eastern Alps, its highest points is 2757m (9,000ft) above sea level but what really makes it special is the 48 hairpin bends that lie before the descending rider as he or she nervously navigates the way down.

From the air, the road looks like a petulant child has angrily thrown a few strands of spaghetti at the mountainside and cyclists adore the Stelvio's complexity and whiff of danger.

But while most are content to work their way cautiously up and down, local boy Giuliano Calore likes to spice things up, and over the years the Italian has attempted and completed a series of mind-blowing stunts on the mountain.

Anticipating the antics of German Christian Adam (see Onward Christian Soloist, page 97), Calore ascended the Stelvio in 1981 playing in turn four different musical instruments, climaxing with an amplified accordion. In 1986 he climbed all 2757m (9,000ft) of the mountain in a time of 2 hours and 20 minutes while it was covered in snow and the temperature was -10°C. Three years later he got to the top once again but this time on a bike lacking both handlebars and brakes.

His undisputed *pièce de résistance*, however, came in 1985 when he sat at the top of the pass seated on another bicycle devoid of both brakes and handlebars. All 48 of the Stelvio's terrifying hairpins hungrily awaited him but Calore refused to back down and set off downwards.

He averaged 80.5kmph (50mph) on the descent, successfully negotiating all the potentially disastrous corners, and just 27 minutes later, he was safely at the bottom having conquered the Stelvio without the luxury of either brakes or steering.

ONWARD CHRISTIAN SOLOIST
1988

The Germans, as a rule, are not renowned for their madcap sense of humour. They've got the whole car manufacturing gig sorted and they're world leaders when it comes to fiscal responsibility but there's a reason why there has never been a Teutonic version of *You've Been Framed*.

Which is, of course, an extremely lazy national stereotype and one which was comprehensively debunked in the 1980s by Christian Adam and his one-man quest to combine his love of music and cycling.

A classically trained violinist, Adam was looking for a new challenge and decided riding his bicycle backwards whilst knocking out a few tunes on his instrument was the next logical step. He would wear his coat and tails for the occasion, he would attach his sheet music to the seat and he would steer the bike while sitting on the handlebars with his bum.

What could possibly go wrong? His first attempt, in 1987, to set a new world record for cycling backwards while playing the violin – a record no-one is convinced actually existed before Adam's bizarre effort – was a humdinger and he clocked up 60.45km (37½ miles) in a time of five hours and nine minutes.

According to Adam, he played J.S. Bach for most of the journey and was particularly impressed with the acoustics he encountered in a motorway tunnel. His second shot in 1988 did not go as smoothly as the first, although by now Adam was clearly getting the hang of the whole reverse cycling challenge and covered a remarkable 113km (70 miles) in just under six hours.

The problem was the very abrupt end to the ride as he collided with a cycling policeman and both men ended up in a rather undignified heap. Luckily for Adam, the dazed copper decided to overlook the myriad of traffic laws he was probably breaking with his silly shenanigans but he did make him pay for the repair of his bike.

With rivals wanting to challenge Adam conspicuous by their absence, there are no further reports of him trying to extend his absurd record.

'ST MICHAEL' TO
THE RESCUE
1990

Lengthy lunch breaks, extra-marital affairs and an innate distrust of the English are as French as the Eiffel Tower. Throw in angry farmers with a political axe to grind and you've virtually got the definition of the French way of life.

French farmers simply love to protest. It's part of the job description and they were in particularly militant mood in 1990 as the wholesale price of their lamb plummeted. The Union Paysanne, the farmers' union, blamed the Government, the Common Agricultural Policy and cheap imports for the drop and there was much muttering and cursing throughout the countryside.

The 1990 Tour de France presented our disgruntled farmers with the perfect opportunity to protest publicly and they'd already got their retaliation in first, disrupting the first day's riding by scattering branches, straw bales and diesel oil along the route.

It was, though, day four, and the 232km (144 mile), rather rural stage, Poitiers and Nantes, that was the real worry. Angry farmers could and probably would be hiding behind every hedge and as the peloton began to pedal slowly out of Poitiers that morning, race director Jean Marie Leblanc was an understandably nervous man.

His anxiety was justified and reports quickly began to filter through that the dreaded agricultural protesters had gathered just outside the village of St-Gemme, 80 km (50 miles) from Poitiers, and were in confrontational mood. Trees had been felled by the side of the road, tyres set alight and there were far too many freshly sharpened pitchforks for comfort.

Leblanc had a decision to make and ordered the riders to stop a few miles short of St-Gemme. It looked like the farmers had won.

They hadn't, however, reckoned with a local teenager by the name of Michael who, according to legend, was appalled by their protest and the unwelcome notoriety it was bringing to his village.

Michael jumped on his little 50cc bike and invited the peloton to follow him on the back roads, bypassing the blockage. The riders accepted and for 32 surreal kilometers (20 miles) before they all rejoined the original route, the Tour was led through the French countryside by a teenager on a scooter.

The farmers were furious, but since their tractors didn't have the pace to catch the peloton, there was absolutely nothing they could do about it.

STAIRWAY TO HEAVEN
1993

Cyclists have two mortal enemies, terrifying twin threats to their riding pleasure which cast long, dark shadows over all that is good and holy about life on two wheels.

The first is the pernicious puncture, the second the heinous hill. Both are as thoroughly unwelcome as the other but while that sudden deflating feeling can be remedied with a well-placed patch and a judicious dab of glue, it's simply impossible to ignore a serious slope or irritating incline.

That was until 1993 when the undulating Norwegian city of Trondheim took pity on its poor, exhausted cyclists and installed the world's first bicycle lift.

Known as the 'Trampe' (the Norwegian for 'to stomp') the lift was beguilingly easy to use. First you bought a key card to activate the mechanism. Then you got into position, placing your right foot on a metal plate that emerged from a concealed conveyor belt and kept your left foot on the pedal. All that was left to do was allow the plate to push you and your bike smoothly up the hill, no sweat, no hassle, no huffing and puffing. Reports of first-time users having a bit of a wobble and tumble were not unheard of but overall the Trampe proved a big hit in Trondheim with locals and tourists alike.

The system was in service for 19 years but in 2012 the city's council decided it was time for an upgrade and Trampe was replaced by 'CycloCable', which was essentially exactly the same but with shinier foot pedals and a new, more expensive logo.

WOMEN, WHEELS & POLITICS
1996

It's easy to be critical of Kim Jong-un. The North Korean dictator is, of course, a basket case who has been single-handedly responsible for ramping up military tensions on the Korean peninsula ever since he got daddy's job in 2012. He's got a dodgy record on human rights, starves his own people and he keeps threatening to blow the world to kingdom come. Overall, definitely a bit of a despotic nutter then.

But what you probably don't realise is that the chubby tyrant is also a committed champion of women cyclists and just three months after succeeding the old man Kim Jong-il as supreme leader, he overturned a bizarre 16-year-long ban on the ladies of North Korea getting into the saddle. Which surely means he can't be all bad.

'In perhaps another sign that North Korean society is changing, Chinese media reported that women are being allowed to ride bicycles for the first time for years,' went the NBC website article. 'Cycling for women was banned in 1996 because the activity wasn't regarded as sufficiently feminine by the male-dominated North Korean regime. It is not clear why the female bicycle ban was reversed but it does appear as though the wheels of change in the country are turning.'

So what Kim's motivation? Chasing the female vote seems unlikely because North Koreans already do exactly as they're told at election time or face the consequences. Maybe he'd just bought shares in the state bicycle company or he was trying to prove he was in touch with his feminine side. Perhaps he was planning a new female bicycle regiment to wage war against the Western oppressors. The truth is, we just don't know.

Sadly North Korea is not alone in discouraging female cyclists and in 2012 the debate in Iran about the morality of women on wheels was reignited when the ultra-conservative Ayatollah Elm Alhuda raged against the dangers of pedal powered sexual equality.

'It is not a sin for a woman to sit on a bicycle saddle, provided she does so indoors or in her backyard,' he said from sometime in the Dark Ages. 'But if she cycles in public her movements and posture will lead to corruption and prostitution.'

Exactly where Alhuda stands on the thorny issue of spin classes is unclear.

TWO WHEELS VERSUS FOUR LEGS
1997

There's a saying about closing the stable doors after the horse has bolted and never has the old adage been more apt or more comical than back in 1997 when an errant steed made an impromptu appearance during the Criterium International race in France, an equine invasion which was thankfully captured by television cameras.

The race was wending its merry way on rural roads near Toulouse when the peloton found itself riding parallel to a field. In said field was our horse who, on spying the riders, began enthusiastically galloping alongside them.

The 'shadow' racing though was short lived as the horse quickly came to the end of its paddock, but rather than call it a day, it leapt a gate and joined the stunned riders on the road. The majority of the peloton fanned out to avoid the unregistered racer but seven competitors were initially unable to pull safely over and for a few hundred metres were forced to look nervously over their shoulders as the four-legged interloper breathed down their necks.

The horse then sprinted to the head of the peloton and overtook the motorbike at the front of the race, inadvertently becoming an unlikely equine pace setter. It could have won, too, but just 19km (12 miles) from the finish it finally realised its *faux pas* and stopped for a bit of a graze.

The live commentary of the incident was almost as hilarious as the images. When the horse began running in the field, the commentators initially found the sight rather endearing but when it vaulted the gate and scattered the riders, they became animated and someone in the studio actually uttered the immortal words 'Ooh la la'. That is absolutely true.

If you're a fan of French cinema all this may sound vaguely familiar as the footage of our friend gatecrashing the Criterium was briefly featured in 2001 romantic comedy *Amélie*, perhaps the greatest equine performance in the movies since *The Godfather*.

AN UNLIKELY MEDICAL HERO
2000

It was not so many pages ago that we learned all about the birth of BMX in America in the early 1970s (see BMX Gets a 'Bum' Deal, page 81) and not long after the craze had gripped the States, it found its way across the Atlantic and a new generation of British kids were suddenly bunny hopping, bar spinning and tail whipping.

One of our leading BMXers back then was a young fella called Tom Lynch, who travelled the world with his bike in the 1980s and won countless individual and team titles. He was seriously good, our Tom.

In 1992 however he decided to get a 'proper' job and joined the London Ambulance Service as a paramedic. He didn't know it then but it was a career move that would eventually revolutionise emergency medical care in the capital and beyond.

Tom quickly got fed up with the notoriously sedate pace of London traffic. His ambulance's flashing blue light was all well and good but Tom, of course, was thinking of a way to getting to his patients as quickly as possible on two rather than four wheels.

'All the time I was thinking how much faster I could get around on my bike,' he explained sensibly. 'But every time I said this to my colleagues, or bosses, they thought I was joking. Eventually I had spoken about it for so long that in 2000 I was allowed to set up a trial run. I knew it would work, all I needed to do was ride a bike fast and do my job when I got there.'

The London Ambulance Cycle Response unit was born and today there are 12 teams working in the capital across the city's 69 ambulance stations. The paramedics ride specially modified Rockhopper bikes and carry 27kg (60lb) of potentially life-saving gear. They cover an average of 40km (25 miles) per shift and have saved an estimated £300,000 per year on fuel bills. In its first decade of operation Cycle Response paramedics treated 50,000 people, freeing up 5000 ambulance hours annually.

'Seven or eight times out of ten, we're arriving on the scene before ambulances purely because we can cut through the traffic,' Lynch said. 'This means that, in about 40 per cent of all cases, we can actually call off the ambulance if the injuries are minor enough, which frees up crews to attend more serious incidents.'

'To be honest, if I have a successful cardiac arrest outcome or hear that someone who I have trained has saved the life of someone who is now walking around healthy, it's the best thing in the world. It's like winning a gold medal every time.'

Cities like Norwich, Cambridge, Leeds, Liverpool and Manchester followed London's lead, as well as cities across the world, and in 2007 Tom's pioneering efforts were recognised when he was awarded an MBE.

Hopefully you were blissfully unaware of the history of two-wheeled triage before reading this but should you ever be grateful for the prompt response of a paramedic on a bike, you now know who to thank.

SIR BRADLEY'S
VEGETARIAN PORKIES
2001

Vegetarianism isn't for everyone. Some people just can't survive on nut cutlets and Quorn alone and for them the allure of the steak and the sausage is simply irresistible. If God hadn't meant us to embrace our inner carnivore, they argue, why did he make certain animals so bloody tasty?

The meat eaters and the veggies rarely see eye to eye and the divide between the two camps presented Sir Bradley Wiggins with an interesting dilemma back in 2001 when he was forced to choose between honesty and the chance to race professionally for the first time.

Wiggo's quandary came when he was invited to ride for the Linda McCartney Racing Team. Set up by Linda and Beatles hubby Paul three years earlier, they'd made history when they became the first British team to enter the prestigious Giro d'Italia and there were big plans to compete at the Tour de France and the UCI World Cup.

The problem was all the team's riders had to be vegetarian. There were to be no exceptions and with Wiggins partial to a Sunday roast and the odd burger, he didn't exactly meet the team's strict criteria. His solution of course was to be as economical as possible with the truth.

'The worst thing about being in the Linda McCartney team was pretending to be a vegetarian,' he admitted in an interview with *The Daily Mail* years later. 'I think everyone was sneaking in the bacon sandwiches.'

Fortunately Wiggins did not have to maintain his dietary deception for long and before he even had the chance to race, the team was suddenly disbanded with reported debts of nearly

£1 million and a dispute with the Union Cycliste Internationale over unpaid riders' wages.

'The whole experience was a disaster, basically a lesson in how not to run a team,' he said. 'It was completely disorganised, the funding wasn't there and you had to be a vegetarian. Instinctively, I ran for home, which in cycling terms meant Team GB, who were fantastic and secured me the Category A Lottery funding again. They could not have been more supportive and they helped ensure that a drama didn't become a crisis.'

It was certainly money well spent as Wiggins famously went on to win the Tour de France in 2012 as well as his fourth Olympic gold medal at the London Games later in the year. He remains a committed carnivore.

MANSER'S AFRICAN ODYSSEY
2003

Africa is a big Continent. Really enormous when you think that, were you to circumnavigate the entire length of the African coastline, you would clock up a staggering 37,000km (23,000 miles).

That's a hell of a lot of pedalling if you were to undertake the epic journey on a humble bicycle, but such trifling obstacles did not deter South African adventurer Riaan Manser when he decided to accept exactly that daunting challenge, an ambitious expedition which very nearly killed him.

Manser set off on his trusty mountain bike from Cape Town in September 2003. He averaged an impressive 88.5km (55 miles) per day and after two years, two months and 15 days in the saddle, travelling through 34 different countries, he had become the first person to circumnavigate Africa on two wheels.

His trek was not without incident. He had to overcome both the heat and humidity of the Sahara and the Libyan deserts, was forced to eat monkey, rat and bat to sustain himself en route and was thrown into jail in Equitorial Guinea after refusing to pay a bribe to border police. He was twice stopped and questioned by Al Qaeda in Algeria, but it was in Liberia where Manser's journey nearly came to a premature and grisly conclusion.

'Our foreign affairs department said they'd withdraw all diplomatic support if I were to enter Liberian territory,' he explained.

'I got into Liberia and I could just sense things were wrong. I walked through a village that had just been burnt out. There were children's toys and suitcases torn open, people's houses and lives destroyed.

'The next day I was pulled off my bicycle in the jungle by guys so high on drugs they were falling around. Then they beat me, 13-year-olds were literally beating me up. Four or five hours later, when they had me in a holding cell, about five or six of them were saying to each other, 'let's gut him, let's kill him, we're wasting time'. I'm a brave guy but my knees were shaking. I realised that that day, 26 February 2004, was the day I was going to die.

'Luckily, I had a magazine with me with our former president Thabo Mbeki's picture in it. One guy recognised the photo and said it was his friend ... and he started laughing. I started laughing with him and 20 minutes later he just said to me out of the blue, "Now go before we kill you". I climbed on my bicycle and got out of there.'

Manser's feat was recognised when he was named 'Adventurer of the Year' by *Out There* magazine in 2006 and granted an audience with Nelson Mandela. He politely declined an offer to work for the Liberian Tourist Board.

THE NUMBERS GAME
2004

A grand total of 219 competitors assembled on the starting line for the Tour de France in 2013 but if you think that's a lot of riders, you've never witnessed the spectacular sight of South Africa's record-breaking Cape Argus Pick 'n' Pay Cycle Tour in full flow.

The 'Argus', as it's known to its friends, regularly attracts over 35,000 professional and amateur cyclists alike and proudly holds the record for the world's largest individually timed race when an incredible 42,614 saddled up and set off on the 109km (68 mile) circular course back in 2004.

The brainchild of friends Bill Mylrea and John Stegmann, the Argus was originally organised as a way to highlight the need for more cycle paths in South Africa and a modest 525 riders turned up for the first race in 1978, pedalling their way from Cape Town, down the Cape Peninsula and back into the city.

Numbers grew steadily over the years and in 1989 the Argus broke through the five-figure barrier for the first time. Six years later they had more 20,000 entrants and by the end of the century there were over 30,000 riders.

The record-breaking year of 2004 saw 42,614 start the race in March and 31,219 complete the course. Italian Antonio Salamone won the men's race in a time of two hours, 32 minutes and 23 seconds while South African Anke Erlank was the fastest woman on the day.

The milestone was officially recognised by *Guinness World Records* and after the Argos organisers decided to cap the number of entrants at 35,000 in 2011, it's a record that could stand uncontested for years to come.

MUDDYING THE WATERS
2005

Mountain bikes are designed for the rough terrain. Going off road is their *raison d'être* and any self respecting mountain bike will positively relish the chance to abandon the namby-pamby tarmac of a pristine highway and get its tyres dirty in the great outdoors.

But even the most testosterone-fuelled bicycle baulks when it hears the dreaded words 'World Mountain Bike Bog Snorkelling Championship', the annual gathering in Wales in which bikes are pushed to their absolute limit. And then a bit more.

First staged in 2005 at the Waen Rhydd Bog near Llanwrtyd, the 'WMBBSC' (as we shall call it for the sake of brevity) is a fiendish test of man and machine and requires a very specific set of modifications before riders are allowed to compete to set the fastest time over two lengths of a 36.5m (40yd), 1.8m (6ft) deep water-filled trench cut through the peat.

Firstly, the air in the bike's tyres has to be replaced with water and the bicycle weighed down by lead weights to avoid competitors experiencing unfair buoyancy. Secondly, and for the same reason, the rider themselves must wear a weighted ruck sack. Thirdly, they must also don a snorkel and diving mask to guard against drowning (and because it looks hilarious).

And then they're off. It's tough work for the competitors as they try to power through the mud and silt and it's not much fun for the bikes either as they spend the entire race submerged under the filthy water.

'It's very murky, you can't see much in the bog and it doesn't taste too good either,' said 40-year-old Bryan Evans from Bridgend after he won the men's competition in a record time of one minute and one second in 2007. 'I'm really relieved that it is over more than anything. You can't really train for this type of event and there is a big element of luck involved because you can go into a pothole and fall over. It's a bit of fun more than anything.'

The true bicycling masochist, however, can go one stage even further and enter the infamous Bog Triathlon at Llanwrtyd which begins with a 19.3km (12 mile) run, two lengths swimming in the peat bog before climaxing with a 40km (25 mile) mountain cycle. Which all sounds like even more, if not exactly clean, 'fun'.

THE FOLD-AWAY PHENOMENON
2006

The first Brompton bike rolled off the production line in London in 1981. The company initially built just 30 of their iconic fold-up cycles but the concept proved hugely popular and today they manufacture over 22,000 bicycles a year, exporting them to more than 40 countries.

They're definitely a design classic and if you don't fancy lugging a unwieldy mountain bike onto a packed commuter train or trying to stuff your 20-speed racer into the boot of a Ford Mondeo, the Brompton is the bike for you.

The only drawback is they're not built for speed. Their 40cm (16in) wheels are never going to enable riders to break the land speed record and practicality rather than alacrity are the watchwords of the company.

But that didn't stop one bright spark coming up with the idea of the Brompton World Championship in 2006, a unique race that sees Brompton enthusiasts from across the world congregating for an annual test of pedal power.

The unusual race was first staged in Barcelona in 2006. Two years later it moved to Blenheim Palace in Oxfordshire and today you can see the world's largest gathering of fold-up bikes at the Orbital Cycling Festival at the Goodwood Motor Circuit.

The rules of the race are simple and endearingly quirky. All competitors must wear a jacket and tie – absolutely no Lycra allowed – and the start sees competitors sprint from a staging area to their bikes, which they must unfold as quickly as possible. It's then on with the serious business of racing over the 15.5km (9½ mile) course (four laps of the motor-racing circuit).

The 2012 event attracted over 800 registrants from 34 countries. As well as prizes for the fastest male and female riders, there are also awards for the best-dressed competitors and the event has proved so popular that spin-off national championships as far afield as Korea, Japan and the USA have sprung up.

Although it's billed as a fun day out, the event also attracts a smattering of professional riders and in 2012 it was Michael Hutchinson, the reigning national champion over 80km (50 miles), was the men's winner with a record time of 20 minutes and 17 seconds.

'It's pretty different,' Hutchinson admitted. 'Most events are a bit more formal but normally a lot smaller in terms of rider numbers. There's a much greater variety of riders. Some competitors are there for a different kind of a day out, some are deadly serious and there are any number of different approaches in between. It is quite a lot more fun than most events.'

WHO LET THE DOGS OUT?

2007

They say a dog is a man's best friend but riders in the Tour de France would disagree vehemently, vulnerable as they are to sudden and unexpected canine incursions onto the route of the race and the carnage that inevitably follows.

One of the most recent examples of a dog-induced crash came in 2007 when Sandy Casar was minding his own business in a breakaway group on the 18th stage of the race when a black Labrador casually emerged from a knot of spectators by the side of the road and cleaned the Frenchman out. Casar inadvertently took down Belgium's Frederick Willems in the process and the pair scrapped to a painful halt.

Casar, however, was nothing if not, ahem, dogged. He picked himself up and despite blood dripping from his right buttock, he amazingly still managed to win the stage. The offending dog couldn't understand what all the fuss was about.

A few days earlier, it had been the turn of German Marcus Burghardt to curse the intervention of one of our four-legged 'friends'. Burghardt was part of the peloton during the ninth stage of the tour when a Golden Retriever ambled innocently in front of him, sending the German rider flying over his handlebars. The portly pooch had obviously been overdoing it on the Pedigree Chum because the impact of the collision buckled Burghardt's front wheel.

Five years later Philippe Gilbert became the latest victim of a canine collision as he rode on the 18th stage from Blagnac to Brive-la-Gaillarde. Once again the dog, an enormous black mongrel, wandered onto the course like he owned the place and the Belgian, plus seven other competitors, hit the tarmac.

Gilbert was steaming. He dusted himself off and marched over to the family who allowed their pampered pooch to stray and gave them a piece of his mind. They responded by cowering silently behind their young daughter.

To add insult to injury, the rider was almost run over by a support vehicle as he turned to rejoin the race. 'His hand has been injured a little as well as his elbow and knee,' said BMC team manager John Lelangue at the end of the day. 'The dog was stronger than him and it won that bout but the important thing is that he could return to his place in the peloton.'

The dog was unavailable for comment.

THE LOVE THAT DARE NOT SPEAK ITS NAME
2007

We all adore our bicycles but it's very important to draw a clear line between affection and infatuation. Letting our feelings for our two-wheeled friends run wild can only end in tears and, in this extreme example, a three-year probationary prison sentence.

Readers of a sensitive disposition are advised to avert their eyes now.

The bizarre bicycle case occurred in Scotland in 2007 when a 51-year-old man called Robert Stewart failed to open his door when cleaners turned up to tidy up his room at a hostel in Ayr. Unfortunately for our man, the cleaners had a job to do and weren't taking no answer for an answer.

'They knocked on the door several times and there was no reply,' prosecutor Gail Davidson told Ayr Sheriff Court at Stewart's rather embarrassing trial. 'They used a master key to unlock the door and they then observed the accused wearing only a white t-shirt, naked from the waist down. The accused was holding the bike and moving his hips back and forth as if to simulate sex.'

Stewart initially claimed it was all a misunderstanding but he knew he was banged to rights and eventually admitted a sexually aggravated breach of the peace by conducting himself in a disorderly manner and simulating sex.

'In almost four decades in the law I thought I had come across every perversion known to mankind,' admitted shocked Sheriff Colin Miller. 'This is a new one on me. I have never heard of a "cycle-sexualist".' Quite, but it seems that bawdy behaviour with bikes is more widespread than we feared and in 2013 there was another incident of two-wheeled titillation.

It happened in the Ostersund area of Sweden and came to light after bike owner Per Edstrom grew tired of finding his tyres punctured on an almost daily basis. He set up a covert camera to shed light on what the hell was going on but perhaps wished he hadn't when he was confronted with graphic images of a man approaching the bicycle, puncturing the wheels and then, ahem, 'enjoying' himself. Manually.

'I am not scared of him, just irritated over all the punctures I have had to fix,' said Edstrom after the shocking discovery. 'This man is probably completely harmless, bicycles are just his thing.'

YOU'VE BEEN FRAMED
2007

There's nothing in the cycling rule book that says the frame has to be made of metal. Alloys of iron, aluminium, titanium and even magnesium are all jolly good materials and while thermoplastics and carbon fibres have tried to muscle in on the metal monopoly in recent years, there are more green solutions.

In 2007, for example, a company called Daedalus Custom Bamboo Bikes unveiled a novel new bicycle constructed from, well, bamboo obviously. It wasn't cheap at over £800 per bike but joint creators Liakos Ariston and Jacob Prinz insisted it had a strength-to-weight ratio to rival some types of steel and that the flexibility of the bamboo offered a remarkably smooth ride.

'We've gained a lot more respect for the material we work with,' said Ariston at the big launch. 'We've had a few accidents on them and generally riders and bikes have come out unscathed.'

The pair drew inspiration from bamboo woodworkers in Thailand but the manufacturing process was not exactly rapid. In fact, the enterprising duo had to let their carefully selected lengths of bamboo 'relax' in their workshop for 18 months before they were ready to be fashioned into a frame, meaning you really had to get your order in early.

Four years after the bamboo bike was unleashed on an unsuspecting world, a Chinese man unveiled a fully functioning cycle crafted almost entirely from lollypop sticks. Only the chain of 35-year-old Sun Chao's creation was not made from sticks and although the ride on the wooden wheels wasn't exactly comfortable, his bizarre creation definitely worked.

Chao got the lollypop building bug after watching a man on television make a model ship for his girlfriend – the man's girlfriend, not our Chao's. He started making his own small-scale models before working up to his magnum opus, the bike. It took 10,000 sticks to make his grand design a reality, although he had the sense to bulk order them rather than licking his way to his required total.

PLUMBING
NEW DEPTHS
2008

We have already heard about the feat of astronaut Alan Bean and his gravity-free pedalling (see Out of this World, page 80) but space is only one of cycling's brave new worlds and in 2008 Vittorio Innocente decided to head in completely the opposite direction, setting a new world record for the deepest underwater bike ride.

The 62-year-old Italian set his bizarre milestone in the waters of Portofino's maritime marine reserve in the Mediterranean on a specially adapted cycle with the tyres filled with water rather than air and 35 kilos of ballast, to prove once again there's nothing someone with far too much time on their hands cannot achieve.

Innocente was lowered into the water by a bemused team of local scuba divers. At a depth of 28m (92ft), he mounted his trusty bike and after nine minutes of submerged pedalling following the route of a natural underwater slope, he had managed to ride down to a depth of 65m (213ft).

In case you're wondering, Innocente *was* equipped with the necessary scuba gear – he's mad, not insane.

'I had to click up a gear to make pedalling easier,' he said, once he was safely back on terra firma and the record had been confirmed by Guinness World Records. 'It was tough because I ran into more mud than I expected.'

Four years after Innocente's idiotic challenge, there was more underwater cycling in evidence when former Royal Marines Chris Sirett and Brian Stokes suddenly decided they had an irresistible urge to set a new record for the longest distance pedalled sub aqua. But before you get too critical, this attempt was done for charity, so give the pair some slack.

Chris and Brian chose the 2012 Southampton Boat Show for their attempt, setting up an exercise bike in a giant, glass-fronted tank and, taking it in turns, got down to business.

Their original target was to clock up 400km (250 miles) in 24 hours but things didn't go quite according to plan and after 15 hours in the tank, they were hauled out after beginning to feel unwell. They did, however, set the record with a total distance of 161km (100.13 miles) covered.

Those of you interested in joining the underwater cycling fraternity are reminded bikes do tend to rust rather rapidly when submerged in water.

THE MADNESS OF SIR DAVE
2008

Dave Brailsford possesses what you might politely describe as an acute eye for detail. Less charitably, you'd have to say the long-serving performance director of British Cycling is an incurable compulsive disorder but the ends justify the means and since his appointment in 2002, he has overseen the emergence of the most successful two-wheeled team in the nation's history.

Sir Dave, as we will temporarily refer to him, is notorious for his meticulousness and from ensuring his riders have the right pillows in their hotel bedrooms to guarantee a revitalising night's sleep to washing their hands correctly to avoid infection and potential illness, the Ubermeister of British cycling has left no stone unturned in his pursuit of success and medals.

He even ordered every single race suit worn by British riders at the Beijing Olympics in 2008 to be shredded in case any rival nations should get their dirty mitts on them and decode the secrets of the material that many believed had played a major role in the team's triumphs.

Team GB's performance in Athens, the Beijing Games four years later and their wonderful performance at London 2012 – amassing a grand total of 18 gold medals in the process – suggests dear old Dave's methods have been nothing but positive in outcome but even he admits he's occasionally trodden a fine line between obsession and utter lunacy.

His potential moment of madness came in the build-up to Beijing Games. Big Dave was pondering the perennial problem of the broken collarbone – the most common injury in cycling – and hit on an innovative (but, of course, secret) form of treatment to get the rider back in the saddle as quickly as possible. All he needed was a willing but appropriately injured guinea pig.

'Ed Clancy [who went on to win gold in the team pursuit] said he would not mind having his two collarbones broken,' Brailsford admitted in an interview in 2009. 'But then, thankfully, someone said "what on earth are you doing?" and this madness was stopped.'

Thank heavens for that. Quite why Clancy was so eager for a trip to the fracture clinic is a mystery but the fact that Brailsford seriously entertained the idea is the real worry. His theories on how best to treat saddle sores really don't bear thinking about.

AIN'T NO SUNSHINE
ANY MORE
2008

Ever since the dawn of time, Man has sought to harness the enormous power of the sun. Swiss scientist Horace-Benedict de Saussure (crazy name, crazy guy) really got the ball rolling in 1767 when he created the first solar collector – an insulated box covered with three layers of glass – and since then, great strides have been made in converting sunshine into something really useful.

William J Bailey (sensible name, sensible guy) moved things on with his 'Copper Collector' in 1908 and in 1970 big business moved in when Exxon (stupid name, dubious environmental record) manufactured the first affordable solar panels. By the time the first prototype solar car was tested in Australia, it looked like we'd cracked it.

Cycling dejectedly lagged behind for years when it came to the sunshine free-for-all but that all looked set to change in 2008 when a London-based design company proudly unveiled their bright yellow 'Cycle Sol', promising it would revolutionise the lives of two-wheeled commuters.

'It is just like an electric bike but the motor runs on a battery that is powered by solar energy,' explained Miroslav Miljevic (tricky name, clever guy), the boffin behind the concept.

> 'There is a large flexible panel on the roof which is covered in solar cells that soak up the sun. You can leave it outside the office during the day to top up the rechargable [battery] ready for the ride home.
>
> 'These days solar cells are pretty good at picking up the lowest amount of light so it should still work when the skies

are cloudy. At night time the small battery can be charged using the mains electricity in just a few hours. I believe it is just what the modern-day commuter needs; it helps you along your way while also being kind to the environment. And if the worst happens and it rains, the roof will keep you dry.'

You've probably seen hundreds, nay thousands of Cycle Sols on the streets of London and other major cities across the country. No? A fundamental design flaw, you say?

Britain, of course, isn't exactly blessed with lashings of sunshine. There's sometimes a couple of weeks in July that aren't absolutely awful but sun drenched we are not, which probably explains why the Cycle Sol hasn't exactly been a big hit. Time, perhaps, for Miroslav to get back to his drawing board.

GOING FOR GOLD
2008

If you're familiar with the TV series *Pimp My Ride*, you'll already be aware that there's no shortage of people with a penchant for customising their cars. The results are invariably a psychedelic nightmare of colour framed with ridiculously big wheels but it makes the owners happy and their probation officers don't seem to mind.

Bicycles, of course, are not immune to a spot of pimping either (see Chicago Defies Convention, page 65) but a Swedish company perhaps got too carried away in 2008 when it built 10 bikes with frames made out of 24-carat gold. Costing an eye-watering £70,000 each, the bicycles were also covered in over 600 Swarovski crystals but if you're worried they were a tad overpriced, they did come with a leather saddle, a 10-year guarantee and the promise of free delivery to any address in the world. So you'd save a bit of the packaging and postage at least.

The gold bikes, however, were positively low rent compared to the two-wheeled offering from artist Damien Hirst, a controversial bicycle that eventually sold at auction for a staggering £325,000.

Hirst had already gained notoriety after pickling a cow, a tiger shark and a sheep in formaldehyde all in the name of art and he continued his one-man assault on the animal kingdom with his bicycle adaptation, taking a Trek Madone model and lacquering the frame with real butterfly wings.

'This is barbaric and horrific,' fumed Sam Glover of People for the Ethical Treatment of Animals. 'Damien Hirst is a one-trick pony. Butterflies are beautiful creatures who should be enjoyed in the wild, not encased in a bike.'

Unsurprisingly Hirst was unrepentant at the time. 'The technical problems were immense as I wanted to use real butterflies and not just pictures of butterflies,' he said. 'I wanted it to shimmer when the light catches it like only real butterflies do and we were trying not to add any extra weight to the bike.'

The bike went for a record £325,000 at Sothebys in New York in 2012 but it's probably safe to assume its value dropped dramatically a few months later.

The bike, you see, was specially designed by Hirst for that Lance Armstrong chap. The disgraced American rider pedalled it during the final stage of the 2009 Tour de France but since he was exposed as cycling's greatest cheat, Armstrong's reputation has nosedived. The bike's value has probably followed a similar trajectory.

COPENHAGEN'S CONGESTED CLAIM TO FAME

2008

The Nirvana for the urban cyclist is a city bereft of beastly cars. It remains more dream than reality for the world's millions of metropolitan riders but as fans of *South Pacific* will be acutely aware, 'if you don't have a dream, how you going to have a dream come true?'

Many places have taken great strides to redress the balance between the internal combustion engine and pedal power but perhaps none more so than Copenhagen, a city which proudly lays claim to the busiest cycling street in the world.

According to local government statistics, 36 per cent of the city's 562,000 residents commute to work by bike every day and an estimated 38,000 of them travel along the 'Noerrebrogade' thoroughfare (that's North Bridge Street for those not fluent in Danish), making it the world's most tyre-treaded urban avenue.

The transformation of Copenhagen into a cycling paradise began in 2008 when the city council closed off the Noerrebrogade to cars for a three-month trial. It all went splendidly despite protests from a few local shopkeepers and at the end of the year, they announced the evil car would be banished forever.

The deluge of new cyclists did, however, present the city with problems and in 2009 they had to introduce a second lane on the Noerrebrogade to accommodate the quicker riders and defuse growing tensions with the more leisurely commuters who now pedal sedately on the inside lane.

A year later, the street had become so popular with cyclists that congestion was becoming a real concern. 'Copenhagen's roads are overloaded with people who want to ride their bicycles in all kinds of weather,' admitted Danish Cyclist Federation spokesman Frits Bredal. 'It's a mode of transportation used by all social classes – even politicians ride bikes.'

The revelation that pesky politicians were taking to two wheels briefly helped to keep numbers down but the council was forced to announce plans for 'super highways' for the city's cyclists, accelerating the process of change and there are now 1000km (62 miles) of bicycle lanes in and around the Copenhagen area.

Car drivers are now firmly in the minority in the Danish capital, a reversal in commuting fortunes which other cities across the world have been watching with interest.

RISING TO THE OCCASION
2008

Doping has sadly scarred the image of professional cycling over the decades but the surprise discovery of a rather unusual haul of drugs during the 2008 Giro d'Italia was the cause for a lot of schoolboy sniggering rather than criminal proceedings and recrimination.

The bizarre story unfolded something like this: A car carrying Natalino Moletta, the father of Italian rider Andrea, from Padua to join up with the race was pulled over by the Old Bill and after a thorough search, they found 82 packets of Viagra, a syringe hidden inside a tube of toothpaste and a portable fridge containing a mysterious fluid.

It initially didn't look good for the Moletta family until someone pointed out that Viagra wasn't actually a banned substance and no laws had technically been broken. Moletta Senior was bailed and the long arm of the law sent off the unidentified liquid for testing.

It transpired it was 'Lutelef', which in tiny amounts can be used as an alternative to Viagra.

The suspicion, of course, was that some cyclists were beginning to use Viagra in some way to boost performance but then some bright spark pointed out a rider was unlikely to use a drug with well-documented 'boosting' qualities while wearing tight Lycra shorts in the full glare of the cameras and thousands of eagle-eyed spectators.

It was a mystery alright. Unsurprisingly, no-one came forward to claim ownership of the famed blue pills and although Moletta was initially suspended by his Gerolsteiner team and pulled out of the Giro, neither he nor his dad were ever charged. Moletta Senior always maintained there was no dodgy plan for the cargo but, equally, never did offer an explanation for why he was in possession of so much Viagra. Mrs Moletta also refused to comment.

THE SUMMIT
OF CYCLING
2009

We have already discussed how cyclists and hills are not natural bosom buddies (see Stairway to Heaven, page 101) but while most amateurs curse the sight of a energy-sapping gradient, some riders actively seek out the big climbs all in the name of adventure.

Two such intrepid souls were Germans Gil Bretschneider and Peer Schepanski who decided to take on Mount Muztagata in the Xinjiang Province of China in 2009 on two wheels, a fearsome 7,546m (24,757ft) slope which is perpetually clad in snow and ice.

The first recorded attempt to climb Muztagata, which translates as 'father of ice mountains', was made by Swedish explorer Sven Hedin back in 1894 but he failed to reach the summit and it was not until 1956 that a team of Chinese and Russian mountaineers finally made it to the top.

Unperturbed, Bretschneider and Schepanski set off on their specially modified bikes with extra-wide tires to combat the treacherous, icy conditions on 23 June, leaving their base camp which sat at an altitude of 5,350m (17,552ft). By 10 July, they had slogged their way to a height 7,211m (23,658ft) and although they could not quite make it all the way up Muztagata, it was still a new milestone for the highest ever bike ride.

A Latvian chap by the name of Bruno Sulcs did reach the peak of the mountain with his bike at his first attempt but pictures of his earlier ascent reveal he *carried* his bicycle on his back rather than pedalling his way up, only getting into the saddle for his rather hair-raising descent. Which was, frankly, missing the point entirely.

In 1996, the late Swedish adventurer Göran Kropp launched a bold attempt to scale Everest without bottled oxygen or the help of

Sherpas and while he was wasn't stupid enough to try to cycle up the world's tallest mountain, he did warm up for the considerable challenge by riding the 12,875km (8,000 miles) from Sweden to base camp.

Kropp set off from Stockholm on 16 October 1995 on his modified mount carrying 108kg (238lb) of equipment and food and finally reached the Himalayas in April 1996.

The Swede got to within 300m (984ft) of the summit on his first attempt before he was forced to turn back. He had to wait three more weeks before he finally stood on top of the world and Kropp celebrated by promptly jumping back into the saddle and cycling part of the way home. Mad doesn't even come close, does it?

BOBBIES ON BIKES
2009

The sight of a police officer on patrol on his bicycle is a common one. Our brave boys and girls in blue / the mindless puppets of a fascist state (covering all political bases there) have long since used two wheels to get the job done and many a criminal has been apprehended thanks to pedal power.

One of the first Forces to turn to bikes in the ongoing war against wrongdoers was the Kent Constabulary, who purchased 20 bicycles at £8 each back in 1896. Just eight years later, they had 129 two-wheel rural patrols operating in the county and the popularity of cycles as an intrinsic part of the bobby's kit, like the truncheon and fabled notebook, quickly spread. Today, London's Metropolitan Police have some 2,500 bicycles at their disposal to keep the streets of the capital free from crime.

There was, however, a bit of a hoo-ha in 2009 about the Old Bill's wheel-mounted divisions when it emerged that perhaps not all their officers were quite as proficient in the saddle as they should be.

The almighty row erupted when the Association of Chief Police Officers (ACPO) announced their intention to publish a 93-page pamphlet entitled *The Police Cycle Training Doctrine*. When it was revealed the booklet would cost thousands of pounds to produce, the Taxpayers' Alliance waded in and questioned the wisdom of spending so much money on a pamphlet which, when you really got down to it, was 'How to ride a bike'. You can't fool the Taxpayers' Alliance, you know.

'I've no doubt that the people behind this are well intentioned but it is bonkers,' fumed the Alliance's spokeswoman Susie Squire. 'I think the booklet is slightly insulting the intelligence of bobbies and you have to ask how necessary this is. We believe that police forces should focus their resources on front-line policing.'

It's easy to see her point. The draft Doctrine contained some real pearls of cycling wisdom, including advice on how to break, to wear padded shorts for 'in-saddle comfort' and a diagram explaining how to tackle particularly tricky junctions. Officers were also warned not to tackle suspects while still 'engaged with the cycle'.

The furore at the perceived profligacy of the police was so intense that London Mayor Boris Johnson decided to have his two-pence worth. 'I think you can do this kind of thing much, much more cheaply,' he told BBC Radio 4's Today programme.

ACPO were forced to admit it was a fair cop and agreed to shelve plans for their bobbies bicycling bible, promising to spend the money saved on new handcuffs and stuff.

IT'LL ALL COME OUT IN THE WASH
2009

Cycling has many purposes including, to name but a fleeting few, getting from A to B quicker than the pedestrians who favour the pavement, getting fit and healthy and, of course, providing grown men with a reasonably credible excuse to wear Lycra in public.

Washing your clothes is not traditionally one of them. Not until 2009, that is, when boffins at the Massachusetts Institute of Technology (MIT) across the pond unveiled the prototype of a revolutionary new device that cunningly combined the joys of cycling and the global dilemma of how to do the weekly laundry.

The premise for the concept was simple. Washing clothes in developing countries can be a bit of a bugger, what with the lack of electricity, water supplies and the latest machine from Hotpoint, and yet pedal power and basic parts, such as discarded oil drums, are readily available.

The eureka moment was almost upon our MIT students and after a brief 15 hours in bed they came up with their 'Bicilavadora' (cleverly combining the Spanish words for bike and washing), a drum mounted on a frame and powered by a bicycle chain. The clothes would get as clean as you were prepared to pedal.

The big selling points of the Bicilavadora were, of course, that it did not need electricity to shift those stubborn stains and the basic parts needed to repair and maintain it could be sourced locally.

The egg heads tested their innovative design in 2009 at an orphanage near Lima in Peru and credit where it's due, it worked an absolute treat. The only problem was convincing the home's resident teenage boys of the need to wash their clothes on a weekly rather than biannual basis.

There are many more, slightly less philanthropic uses of pedal power. In 2012 the Cottage Lodge hotel in the New Forest installed a bicycle-powered television in one of its rooms, and it's now possible to buy a static bike with a blender attached to the handlebars should, presumably, you have an insatiable urge for a mango and passion fruit smoothie while in the saddle.

In 2013, however, American Edward Belden took it a step even further when he opened an ice-cream parlour, the 'Peddler's Creamery', in Los Angeles, freezing all of his delicious homemade offerings by pedal power alone.

'Bicycling is something I've been interested in since I was a kid,' Eddie panted. 'And I've been into ice cream since high school. My first job was at a Baskin-Robbins. I've been trying to figure out how to put those things together.'

If the idea was to catch on and customers forced to freeze their own 99s, America could be well on its way to solving its growing obesity crisis.

BATTERIES NOT INCLUDED
2010

An essential part of the bicycle's DNA is the reliance on human power. Bikes come in many different shapes and sizes but our two-wheeled friends are united in their contempt for anything resembling an engine. Nature may abhor a vacuum but cycles absolutely hate motors.

Which is why the world of professional cycling was rocked to its foundations in 2010 when high-profile Swiss rider Fabian Cancellara was accused of using a motor concealed in his bike frame to help him win the Tour of Flanders and the Paris–Roubaix race.

The accusation of what amounted to racing heresy was made by former professional rider Davide Cassani. He stated in a video posted on YouTube that a small motor could easily be hidden in the seat tube of a bike and the ignition switch located in the handlebars and then showed clips of Cancellara in action, claiming there were moments his dramatic increases in speed could only have been achieved with, ahem, 'extra help'.

The indignant Swiss was quick to rebuff the accusations. 'In fact it was pretty funny at first but it is such a big story that it's no longer the case,' he told the Belgian newspaper *Het Nieuwsblad*. 'It's a sad story and really outrageous. Don't worry, my accomplishments are the result of hard work. It's so stupid I'm speechless. I've never had batteries on my bike.'

The problem was there were already rumours of unnamed riders using a new engine called the Gruber Assist which could surreptitiously generate 100 watts of additional power and when the Cancellara 'story' broke, fear mixed with suspicion and everyone got rather hot under the collar.

It's important to stress here that the governing body, Union Cycliste Internationale (UCI), decided Cancellara was innocent and refused to investigate the unproven slurs but the allegation alone raised the spectre of motorised cheating in a sport that was still wrestling with the ongoing issue of doping.

The worrying aspect of the tale was the realisation that the authorities were in no real position to catch out potential 'motor cheats'. 'If there's been some kind of fraud, there's no way of proving it,' admitted the UCI's technical chief Jean Wauthier. 'Certainly we're going to have to speed up our research so we can scan all competition bikes in a quick and efficient way. Up till now, such controls simply haven't been used.'

BROUGHT DOWN TO EARTH
2011

It was back in 1973 that Alan Bean enjoyed his unprecedented pedal in space (see Out of this World, page 80) but fellow astronaut Tim Kopra found bicycling and going into orbit far less compatible 38 years later when he was left to curse his love of two wheels.

A former Army helicopter pilot and veteran of both the American campaigns in Iraq, Kopra was part of the crew that blasted off in the Endeavour shuttle in July 2009, spending three months aboard the International Space Station.

Almost as soon as he touched down, he was selected for the mission on Discovery in February 2011 and he also got the nod to make the two space walks scheduled for the trip. A popular boy, our Tim.

After 20 months of intensive, arduous training and three threats of divorce from his lonely, disgruntled missus, Kopra was in tip-top shape and ready for lift-off.

Five weeks before the big day, however, Tim made the fateful decision to go out for a nice relaxing bike ride which ended with him breaking his hip. NASA refused to release details of exactly what happened or what he hit but Kopra's big adventure was over.

The shuttle, of course, could not be delayed, NASA turned to the sub's bench and they left on schedule and without him.

'It was obviously a disappointment for Tim to not be available for this upcoming launch window,' said chief astronaut Peggy Whitson after hearing the news, 'but he understands very well that we have to be prepared to fly.'

To rub salt into the wound, the shuttle that Kopra missed was the STS-133. The iconic aircraft made just two more trips into space before it was retired by NASA in 2011, meaning accident-prone Tim will now never get the chance to go up in the shuttle again.

THE HEIGHT OF INGENUITY
2012

Cycling has proved a fertile area for those whose mission in life is to see their names in *Guinness World Records*. Getting into the famed book is a moot claim to fame when you consider Britain's Steve Mesure made the grade in 2013 after creating the world's biggest whoopee cushion while Croatia's Krunoslav Budiselic was included after his Herculean achievement of fitting 150 socks on his right foot (we're honestly not making this up) but, hey, it still beats train spotting as a hobby.

The number of record-breaking feats you can accomplish in the saddle is almost limitless and then there's also extreme bicycle modifications, building bigger, longer, faster or heavier bikes than ever seen before in an attempt to join the 'elite' *Guinness World Records* club.

In 2012 a Cuban chap called Felix Guirola decided to make his bid to become a bicycle record breaker. Felix opted for the 'world's tallest bike' category and after months toiling away with his blow torch in a workshop in Havana, he proudly emerged with his creation, a 5.5m (18ft) high monster that would give the faint-hearted rider severe vertigo.

'I've never been much of a cyclist,' Felix confessed, 'but I really like riding tall bikes. I don't know if this interests Cubans but it interests me. This is my hobby.' His other half was noticeably less enthusiastic. 'I say sometimes it's like an obsession,' Mrs Guirola said through gritted teeth. 'It is always about bicycles and each passing day it gets a little bit taller.'

Marital tensions aside, Felix's should have been on cloud nine but his face dropped when someone pointed out to him that, according to *Guinness World Records*, the tallest bike was actually 5.5m (18ft 2½in), a behemoth built by Canadian pastor Terry Goertzen and ridden without stabilisers over a distance of 300m (328 yards) at the North Kildonan Mennonite Brethren Church in Winnipeg in 2004.

'Nobody ever told me anything,' replied a clearly dejected Felix as he scurried off to his workshop clutching more metal piping and his trusty blow torch.

Other oversized, record-breaking bikes include the extraordinarily elongated beast built by members of the Mijl Van Mares workers collective in the Netherlands in 2011, a cycle that measured a staggering 35.8m (117½ft) from front wheel to back, while it's a case of double Dutch when it comes to the heaviest ever cycle, a 750kg (1,653lb) whopper constructed by Wouter van den Bosch in Arnhem.

'I've always been fascinated by mechanics and building things,' said Wouter. 'I was offered this huge tractor tire, then thought, "what can I make using this?"'

Most people would have opted for a sandpit for the kids.

THE BIG CHILL
2012

Cyclists and snow are rarely happy bedfellows. Even the most devoted rider will think twice about setting out for an invigorating pedal on a winter's morning if, on drawing the bedroom curtains, they're confronted by masses of the white stuff. Bikes are tough but even they would follow the birds south for the winter if they had a choice.

Which is why, until 2012 at least, successive generations of intrepid explorers had never deigned to use our two-wheeled friends en route to the South Pole, opting instead to load up with Winalot and let the husky take the strain.

It all changed, however, in the name of *Sport Relief* when Blue Peter presenter Helen Skelton embarked on an ambitious, 800km (500 mile) expedition into the wintery wilderness of Antarctica for charity, 166km (103 miles) of which our indomitable children's TV presenter planned to travel in the saddle.

'I've lost count of the number of people who have told me a push bike won't work in Antarctica and that I am setting myself up for a fall,' she confessed before pulling on her thermals and setting off. 'It's become a joke among the Icelandic Arctic truck drivers who provide logistical support here. They think I am bonkers.'

Braving temperatures as low as minus 48°C, Helen began her bid to reach the South Pole on 4 January and it soon became apparent the truckers might have a point.

'We had a ten-hour day yesterday with the bikes,' she recorded in her diary for the *Daily Telegraph*.

> 'The first part of the day went well. We covered 10 miles quite quickly then we hit some soft snow and that was game over for the bikes. We ended up pushing them for the last six miles to make sure we made the miles for the day. This

morning the snow conditions were no better so we had to push our bikes again, not what you need in minus 23 as you get colder quicker. So we took the decision to swap onto the skis, but progress has been slow, mainly as I'm not much of a cross-country skier.

'The hardness of the snow the nearer you get to the Pole gets softer. In fact its texture, in parts, is just like sand and the bike wheels simply can't get any traction or grip.'

Helen, though, was nothing if not plucky and after 18 days in the freezer she finally reached the South Pole, proudly pedalling the final few miles just to prove a point to the sceptics.

PLAY YOUR CARD RIGHT
2012

It's all well and good manufacturing a bicycle frame from bamboo (see You've Been Framed, page 121) but the process still involves the massacre of an innocent plant, cruelly cut down in its prime. The green credentials of the bamboo bike are moot.

It would surely be far more environmentally friendly if we could avoid such carnage and rather recycle what we have already harvested from the natural world. An affordable, recycled cardboard bicycle maybe?

Thank god then for Israeli-based engineer Izhar Gafni and his backers ERB who unveiled just such a wondrous contraption in 2012 with the bold promise their prototype was going to change the world.

'Like Henry Ford who made the car available to anybody,' enthused Gafni, 'this bike is going to be cheap and available to any child in the world, including children in Africa who walk dozens of miles to school every day.'

Big words but you've got to hand it to Gafni and his friends, who did, indeed, manage to layer and form the recycled cardboard in such a way it was strong enough to carry the weight of an adult. Not a morbidly obese giant, admittedly, but a normal-sized grown-up nonetheless.

The design team also successfully negotiated the nagging problem that cardboard has a tendency to get soggy in the rain, coating the frame of their bike with a waterproof resin before applying a fetching coat of paint. Job done.

Each bike cost just £10 to manufacture and everyone connected to the project was jolly pleased.

'The biggest challenge of the Cardboard Bike Project was to learn and develop a whole new know how of cardboard,' an ERB spokesman gushed. 'The challenge was to take the cardboard material and pass it through a set of treatments to replace the raw materials of plastic, wood or metal.' Nothing is impossible if you have patience and you are persistent.

'Cardboard technologies is all about making a better world for us to live in by two main principals: creating the ability to produce almost any daily product from at least 95 per cent recycled materials and building auto production lines with a simple post-production assembly that will be performed by people with difficulties or disabilities.'

The day when cyclists can build their own bikes at home from empty cornflake boxes or discarded All Bran packets may be some way off just yet but it's a tantalisingly prospect.

JUST MARRIED!
2012

The honeymoon is traditionally a long overdue opportunity for the newlywed couple to have some precious time alone, recover from the trials and tribulations of organising their recent nuptials, forget about how much money they've just wasted on champagne and vol-au-vents and slag off their new in-laws.

It's also, perhaps, a once-in-a-lifetime opportunity for some personal pampering and indulgence before reality bites, the patter of tiny feet deafens and the happy couple are inevitably reduced to emotional, physical and financial wrecks.

And yet not all new couples conform to the convention. After tying the knot, Londoners Kat and Steve Turner turned their back on luxury hotels and sun loungers and set off on an epic, potentially record-breaking tandem ride from New Zealand to London.

Worryingly, Kat had never ridden a bike for more than a few yards before embarking on the bizarre matrimonial challenge but after a few, quick lessons the Turners set off in May 2012 from Christchurch and by the end of the year, they'd reached Darwin and the north coast of Australia.

'The first four months of this trip were so hard,' Kat admitted. 'We cycled through gallons of rain and waves of gales. My feet felt like they were constantly soaked and at times I wanted to give up so much, so that I could enjoy a beer and good company with friends or the warmth of a fire or a Sunday roast at mum's or a belly-aching laugh with my brother or a family knees-up in Plymouth. And, dare I say it, even working in a dry office felt appealing at times.'

A few angry dogs, giant lizards and hungry rats slowed their initial progress but after beginning the Asian leg of their grand tour, Mr and Mrs finally felt they were getting to grips with the task. If not each other.

'At first we were not sure whether we could do what we were planning to do but now that we have completed six months and the Australian Outback we feel much more confident that we can do this,' said Steve. If we do, it will be the most amazing achievement. We have found the first months very hard and we haven't had the energy or the contacts to do very much other than cycle, which isn't exactly a traditional way of enjoying a honeymoon.'

The couple hope to eclipse the previous tandem world record of 38,143km (23,700 miles) set by Britain's Phil and Louise Shambrook in 1997 who, for the record, were not on honeymoon during their own mammoth effort. At the time of going to press, the happy but exhausted Turners were somewhere in Georgia and hope to finally return to the UK sometime in 2014.

They have promised to write their 'thank you' cards as soon as they get back.

JAMIE'S ROAD
TO NOWHERE
2012

Static bikes are a contentious issue in the cycling community. Traditionalists fume that pedalling without actually moving anywhere is an aberration, an affront to the very essence of cycling, while forward-thinking two-wheel devotees counter that it beats getting chased by dogs or knocked over by idiots in BMWs.

Others, such as tennis coach Jamie McDonald, eagerly embrace both disciplines.

Jamie began 2012 on something of a mad mission. His first challenge began in January when he and his trusty bike set off from the Thai capital Bangkok, his ambitious aim to reach his hometown of Gloucester by pedal power alone. It took him 10 months to cycle the 22,530km (14,000 miles) back to the UK, but after a journey which took him through Iran and Iraq to name but two of the more dangerous countries he traversed, Jamie arrived home safely.

Most sane people would have enjoyed a well-earned spot of R&R after completing such a feat but Jamie was restless and less than a month after his return he decided to target the world record for continuous pedalling on a static bike, a remarkable milestone of 224 hours, 24 minutes and 24 exhausting seconds set by Patrizio Sciroli of Italy in 2011.

In December, he strapped himself on and began pumping his legs once again. The rules stated he had to cycle for a minimum of 22 hours per day at an average of 12mph but the masochist in Jamie was in evidence one more as he limited himself to just 90 minutes sleep rather than the two hours he was allowed.

After 10 days in the saddle, he had smashed Sciroli's record but powered on and eventually set a new mark of 290 hours and 18 minutes on the bike. 'I've been cycling for 11 days straight, am I hallucinating?' he gasped when it was all finally over. 'No, this is for real. This is just mind blowing.'

In September 2013 *Guinness World Records* got in touch to confirm Jamie's ordeal had officially made the book but he wasn't at home to receive the good news, indisposed as he was on a coast-to-coast run across Canada – the potentially suicidal equivalent of 200 marathons in just 275 days – in an attempt to set another record.

The expression 'glutton for punishment' doesn't even come close.

CARRY ON, DOCTOR
2012

Bicycles boast a long, proud history of aiding the medical profession from their deployment on the bloody battlefields of World War One, their tireless work with dowdy district nurses in remote, rural areas to the modern cycle response units which today reassuringly patrol our cities (see An Unlikely Medical Hero, page 106).

A more unlikely and comical collaboration between a bicycle and the medical community, however, came to light in the American state of Louisiana in 2012 when a Dr Catherine Baucom, a dedicated oncologist, suddenly found herself in rather desperate need of some two-wheeled assistance.

A surgeon at a hospital in the state capital of Baton Rouge, Doc Baucom set off for work as usual one sunny morning in August. She drove onto the Interstate but a pile-up a few miles up the road prematurely curtailed her journey and she found herself stuck in traffic. Due in surgery and with the clock ticking, an increasingly anxious Baucom decided to pull off the Interstate and drive to a nearby friend's house.

Luckily her pal did have an alternative form of transport but it turned out to be his seven-year-old daughter's pink bike, complete with a pink Disney helmet. Remembering her Hippocratic Oath, Baucom didn't blink an eye and before you could say stabilisers, she was back on the road and pedalling furiously towards the hospital.

At six foot, our unstoppable doctor wasn't exactly well suited to her new ride but she persevered and after a couple of miles of uncomfortable cycling she came across a police patrol which had been despatched to manage the aftermath of the Interstate accident. 'I rode up on this bright pink bike wearing a princess helmet,' Baucom said. 'They probably thought I was a mental patient. I said, "Look, I've got to operate, can you let me through?"'

They did and 'escorted' Baucom safely and on time to the operating theatre, the climax of a frenetic rush to surgery. It would have been less frantic had the police actually given her a lift to the hospital rather than following her and her pint-sized bike with their lights flashing.

FROOME'S AFRICAN ADVENTURE
2013

We've already enjoyed a few laughs at the expense of the Tour de France riders who've had the misfortune to be involved in canine collisions in the past (see Who Let The Dogs Out?, page 117) but our four-legged friends wouldn't have worried 2013 Tour champion Chris Froome, judging by his own experiences of the animal kingdom growing up in Africa.

The Team Sky star was raised in the rural highlands north of the Kenyan capital Nairobi and a misplaced pooch would have been a picnic compared to the far more fearsome African beasts he regularly encountered in his formative years.

The sight of wild lions on the prowl while he was out training was a common one for the youngster but it was a disgruntled hippopotamus that came closest to bringing Froome's career to a premature end. 'Growing up in Africa has its colourful times,' he said in 2011. 'I was fishing one day and a hippo came out of the river and chased me up an embankment. To most people in Europe, it's something so foreign. There are many places in Africa I've been riding my bike and you come across animals.'

The danger did not only lurk outdoors and a slither of snakes billeted at the family house mercifully never turned on the future Tour champion. 'Mum wasn't a fan but wanted to encourage us learning, so she let us keep them in the house,' recalled older brother Jeremy. 'We had about 50 in the house. Chris had two pythons, Rocky and Shandy, he absolutely loved.'

The animal kingdom, however, was not the only threat to the teenager. The fields around the family home were riddled with bilharzias, a debilitating parasitic infection that can affect growth in children and Froome and both his brothers suffered bouts of the disease growing up.

And then there were the manmade hazards, including concealed metal spikes and HGVs.

The metal spike went right through his foot during a family holiday. 'It needed a hacksaw to cut it off and though it must have been excruciatingly painful,' said Jeremy. 'He never complained, just stayed quiet. That's Chris. People see a quiet, polite soul but inside he's fiery and strong.'

The lorries were more fun as Froome hung onto the back of the speeding trucks while out on his bike but it is something of a minor miracle he never hit one of the numerous potholes or dead dogs and finish his ride lying in a ditch.

Compared to these childhood challenges, winning the Tour probably seemed like a breeze.

THE SKY'S THE LIMIT
2013

We have already explored the bicycle's key role in helping man get airborne at the start of the 20th century (see The Wright Stuff, page 30) but in recent years the cycling fraternity has been making a concerted effort to muscle in on the aeroplane's dominance of the skies.

The concept of a flying bike had tantalised and teased frustrated inventors for decades but in 2013 it finally became a reality when two British designers unveiled their 'Paravelo', an innovation which they boldly promised would revolutionise commuting forever.

Powered by a large fan connected to a bio-fuel engine and mounted on two extra, supporting wheels at the back of the bike, the Paravelo achieved lift-off courtesy of a parachute attached to the frame. It wasn't a million miles away from a microlight and video evidence proved it definitely could fly.

'We live in Kingston upon Thames on the outskirts of London, two minutes walk from the birthplace of the Sopwith Aviation Company, which built the Sopwith Camel for the Royal Air Force during the First World War,' explained co-creator John Foden. 'We were enchanted by the connection between cycling and the birth of powered flight. The Wright brothers were former bicycle mechanics, so we designed the Paravelo to recapture that pioneering era.'

Foden and his fellow boffin Yannick Read claimed their machine could reach heights of 1219m (4,000ft) and stay airborne for up to three hours. It could also be folded up and stored, they enthused, meaning you could fly to work and then pop your Paravelo away neatly in the stationary cupboard. They were less forthcoming when asked what the hell you'd do should you find yourself 609m (2,000ft) above Grimsby town centre on a Tuesday morning and the engine stalls.

In the same year, a group of Czech chaps with white coats took a very different approach to the old 'flying bike' conundrum when they unveiled a prototype that did away altogether with the parachute and instead gained elevation thanks to a series of six downward facing fans welded to the cycle's frame.

They demonstrated their invention to reporters but rather worryingly did not have sufficient faith in their machine to put a real life person in the saddle and flew the bike by remote control.

'Our main motivation in working on the project was neither profit nor commercial interest,' explained Ales Kobylik, 'but the fulfilment of our boyish dreams.'

Questions about safety features and the possibility of suffering a horrible death, however, were met with an embarrassed silence and until some genius can come up with the answers, the future of flying bikes seems uncertain at best.

THE NEED FOR SPEED
2013

Ever since the modern bicycle emerged in the late 19th century, people have been endeavouring to go faster and faster and then even faster still on two wheels. The pursuit of speed has, of course, resulted in countless crashes but it's also produced some amazing feats of engineering and moments of sheer, undiluted madness.

The maddest of them all in the cycling speed stakes has to be Frenchman Francois Gissy, who clocked up a potentially fatal but admittedly impressive 163mph on his hydrogen-peroxide powered rocket bike in 2013, a new land speed record on a bicycle.

To put it into context, that's faster than the winner of the 3.30 at Kempton, an Andy Murray first serve or an Audi RS6 flat out. It's even faster than a politician on the campaign trail after they've just spotted a baby and a photographer in close proximity.

Gissy built his bike himself and then attached a reinforced storage tank filled with liquid hydrogen peroxide which, when mixed with a catalyst, produces oodles of steam which in turn provides the thrust. A GPS tracker on the handlebars recorded the ridiculous speed.

The Munchhouse Aerodrome in Alsace, France, provided the setting for the attempt and after ensuring his will was in order and saying a few Hail Marys, Gissy flipped the switch and duly rocketed into the record books.

There's a problem though, isn't there? A rocket-powered bike doesn't exactly adhere to the principles of pedal power and while he didn't technically convert his bicycle into a motorbike, his feat was not a muscular achievement.

The real distinction as the fastest man on two wheels, unadulterated by rockets, unaided by a tow from a fast car and without the help of a slipstream created by an advance vehicle, therefore belongs to Dutchman Sebastian Bowier.

Superb Seb set his record in September 2013 at Battle Mountain in Nevada in a specially designed recumbent bike shielded by an aerodynamic shell covered in the same coating used on Formula One cars, clocking an incredible top speed of 83.13mph courtesy of pedal power alone.

Bowier's amazing effort eclipsed the previous record set by Canadian Sam Whittingham four years earlier but it was an unbelievably close run thing, the Dutchman going just 0.311mph faster than his rival.

SHANGHAI HIGH RISE

2013

The Chinese have become addicted to building skyscrapers. They just can't get enough of throwing up yet taller and taller buildings, towering architectural reminders to the rest of the world that they'll be in charge soon and we'd better not forget it. Thank you.

The imposing Shanghai World Financial Centre – an enticing blend of office space, shops and a luxury hotel – first opened its doors for business in 2008. At the time of the grand unveiling, it was officially the second tallest building in the world but that didn't last long and by 2013 it was a mere fifth on the list.

Still, an impressive erection nonetheless (stop giggling at the back). One hundred and one floors, a dizzying 492m (161ft) tall and an impossible 2,754 steps just to get the breathtaking observation deck on the 100th floor. You would have to be mad to even attempt it on foot.

Or, of course, on two wheels but pedalling up skyscrapers is Krystian Herba's thing and in March 2013 the part-time Polish PE teacher, part-time stunt rider pitched up at the SWFC (as the locals call it) ready for his latest challenge.

He'd already knocked off the comparatively puny Rose Rayhaan building in Dubai – a mere 2040 steps over 91 floors – and now he'd come to show Shanghai what he could really do.

Now it's important to put this challenge, the kind of superhuman feat that *Guinness World Records* will actually recognise, into context. Herba is not allowed to put his feet down for the duration of the attempt and he's not allowed to touch the walls with his hands either. He simply has to keep pedalling up and up and up. On a bike with no seat, lest it unbalance him.

Impossible? Not for our Krystian, who successfully pedalled, bounced and balanced his bike all the way to the SWFC's 100th floor in a time of one hour, 21 minutes and 53 seconds.

'It is like asking a Himalayan climber why he is going to the mountains if he can simply stay at home,' Herba replied when quizzed why the hell he spent his spare time climbing skyscrapers on his bike. 'It's the strength and desire to be better and faster and to overcome, not only another record, but also weaknesses.'

That or he's claustrophobic and won't take the lift.

THE BICYCLE BANDITS
2013

We have already discussed how over the years law enforcement has taken to two wheels to catch crooks (see Bobbies on Bikes, page 136) but the criminal fraternity are also aware of pedal power, as these contrasting tales of audacious crooks prove.

There are, somewhat worryingly, countless stories of armed robberies in which the perpetrator makes his or her escape on a bike but one of the most surreal was the stick-up at a branch of Bank of America in Georgia in 2013, a raid carried out by a man wearing a bright blonde wig. Inconspicuous is not the word that springs to mind.

'I noticed him right away' said one customer after the robbery, 'because when I walked in, I saw him sitting there. He had on the wig and he just kind of looked like a transsexual.'

The crook's disguise may have been poor but what it lacked in subtlety, he made up for with audacity and after grabbing a bag of cash, he calmly strolled out of the building and got into the saddle for a successful getaway. An oblivious security guard at the bank even held the door open for him as he made his exit.

The two-wheeled thief who targeted a Wells Fargo bank in Alaska two years earlier was not nearly so lucky. Things initially went to plan but after leaving the bank with his ill-gotten gains, he was spotted pedalling away by a patrol car and the Old Bill gave chase. The crook made it a little further but the game was up when the officer manoeuvred his car in front of the fleeing bicycle and the criminal was sent unceremoniously crashing over the bonnet.

'He ended in a heap with his money pouring out of his pack,' revealed Lt. Dave Parker. 'It didn't hurt him at all. He popped up and ran away.'

It was merely a temporary reprieve as the officer popped on his running shoes, chased the suspect down and slapped on the cuffs.

Natural hazards, however, can be as dangerous a police cars, as one criminal found out in 2009 when he walked into a Canadian petrol station near Niagara Falls wielding a butcher's knife and demanded the money.

The attendant wisely paid up but when the thief made off on his bicycle, he jumped into his car and followed him. The crook panicked and the bizarre game of cat and mouse came to an abrupt and painful end when he crashed head first into a tree.

The most idiotic attempt to escape justice on two wheels, though, has to be the American man who walked into a Wal-Mart in Florida in 2012 and half inched an 80cm (32in) plasma TV, jumped on his bike and began pedalling. His new acquisition proved to be more hindrance than help and, unable to steer properly, he slammed into a police car and was promptly nicked.

IT'S NOT ALWAYS
GOOD TO TALK
2013

One of cyclists' perennial gripes about motorists is their persistent and illegal use of mobile phones. It's impossible for drivers, they argue, to give the road their due care and attention while they're being bombarded by calls about PPI, arguing with their other halves or trying to order a pepperoni pizza.

It was back in 2003 that the UK banned the use of handheld mobiles behind the wheel but other countries have gone even further to curtail potentially dangerous conversations on the road and in certain states in Australia it also illegal to use your mobile while in the saddle.

It's a tough law but one that is enforced, as an anonymous female cyclist in a suburb of Adelaide discovered in 2013 when the eagle-eyed Old Bill spotted her chatting away on the phone while riding a bike. She was fined $110 for her two-wheeled transgression and sent on her way.

Hardly a 'strange tale' you cry but we haven't yet touched upon the bike on which she committed her heinous crime, a homemade, multicoloured double decker contraption which really was a sight to behold.

Boasting a yellow 'lower' frame with a bright pink 'upper' frame *avec* wheels precariously welded on top, the cycle was powered by a long chain running at 45 degrees between the chain wheel at the top and the 'cassette' (the little 'toothy' metal circle) at the bottom rear. It was all topped off with some fetching beads cunningly woven between the spokes of the front wheel and looked as psychedelic as it did potentially lethal.

'Cyclists are vulnerable road users,' intoned a straight-faced police spokesman after the unnamed woman was pulled over, 'and are reminded that the road rules also apply to them.'

How our cyclist actually managed to ride her bizarre bike *and* speak on the phone is something of a mystery but perhaps she opted for her elevated pedalling position in order to get a better reception on her mobile.

CANADIAN
CARDBOARD CAPER
2013

Theft is the scourge of the urban cyclist's life, transforming a brief stop-off for a cinnamon latte and croissant into a heart-rending experience as they emerge from Costa to discover their beloved wheels have disappeared.

The chances of successfully recovering their prized possession are usually as remote as Bouvet Island (look it up on a map) and while it might be unfair to suggest that the police don't prioritise searching for pilfered bikes, you'd definitely get laughed out of the station if you popped in and demanded to speak to the head of the crack Cycle Crime Unit.

Occasionally, however, the scales of justice do tip in the favour of the wronged rider, emotional reunions between man and machine do happen and stolen bikes are found.

One such serendipitous conclusion was reached in Toronto in 2013 when yet another bike was criminally separated from its lock and promptly nicked. The owner held out little hope of ever seeing it again but a few days later his friend – get this, a bicycle mechanic – spotted the missing bike chained to a metal post on the side of the street and through the wonderful medium of the Internet (or, more specifically, the Reddit website) announced to his mate and the wider world that bikey was coming home.

The pair set about cutting the bike free from its new lock but rather than call it a day, they decided to rub their victory in the thief's face, leaving a cardboard cut out of a bicycle in the exact same spot with a note attached.

'Dear Bike Thief,' it read. 'You rascal! You took my bike earlier this week and forgot to tell me where you'd leave it! It took a stroke of great luck that my friend, who's also my bike mechanic, happened to spot it right here. Isn't that crazy? Anyway, I kinda need my bike so I'm taking it back. Please accept this substitute until you can afford your own. Cheers!'

BIBLIOGRAPHY

BOOKS

Cycling's Greatest Misadventures, edited by Erich Schweikher & Paul Diamond, Casagrande Press, 2007

Guinness World Records 2013, editor-in-chief Craig Glenday, Guinness World Records Limited, 2013

The Official Tour de France Records, Chris Sidwells, Carlton Books Limited, 2012

Cycling's 50 Craziest Stories, Les Woodland, McGann Publishing, 2010

Muck, Sweat & Gears, Alan Anderson, Carlton Books Limited, 2011

The Bluffer's Guide To Cycling, Rob Ainsley, Bluffers, 2013

French Revolutions: Cycling the Tour de France, Tim Moore, Yellow Jersey, 2012

Cyclepedia: A Tour of Iconic Bicycle Designs, Michael Embacher & Paul Smith,
Thames & Hudson, 2011

The History of Cycling in Fifty Bikes, Tom Ambrose, The History Press Limited, 2013

The Story of the Tour de France, Bill McGann & Carol McGann, Dog Ear Publishing, 2006

WEBSITES

history.nasa.gov

www.cyclejumpers.com

www.nbcnews.com

www.topendsports.com

www.news-herald.com

www.brompton.co.uk

www.oxfordtimes.co.uk

www.myorangebrompton.com/

www.bicycle-and-bikes.com

ftp.cyclingnews.com

www.bikeradar.com

www.riaanmanser.com

www.bmxultra.com

www.crazyguyonabike.com

bicycling.about.com

www.ibike.org

www.bikereader.com

www.biography.com

For your reading pleasure

THE
STRANGEST
SERIES

The *Strangest* Series has been delighting
and enthralling readers for decades with
weird, exotic, spooky and baffling tales of
the absurd, ridiculous and the bizarre.
This bestselling range of fascinating books –
from the Ashes to Fishing, Football to London
and Motor Racing to the World Cup, detail the
very curious history of each subject area's
funniest, oddest and most compelling
characters, locations and events.
For all things weird and wonderful, pick up a
Strangest from www.anovabooks.com today…

9781861052933

9781861055354

9781907554087

9781861051844

9781905798162

9781861054111

9781861057457

9781861056795

9781907554339

9781861059765

9781861058270

9781907554131

9781861059383

9781906032906

9781905798285

AND NOW FOR SOMETHING EVEN STRANGER!

9781906032760   9781906032913   9781907554476

The Strangest Series has now introduced even stranger delights for its readers. With *The Ashes' Strangest*, *World Cup's Strangest* and *Olympics' Strangest*, fans of this unique and extraordinary series can delve even deeper into the world of the bizarre and utterly ridiculous with these special sport-related *Strangests*. A great read no matter where you are, these fascinating books highlight the bizarre, weird and downright bonkers events, characters and locations of each particular sport.

Just don't read them all at once though – you might start acting all peculiar! You have been warned.